Divorced As F*
IN SEVEN SPIRITUAL STEPS

Bernadette Purcell LCSW

Treehouse Publishing 2022

Treehouse Publishing
Middletown, NJ 07748
United States

First edition

Printed in the United States of America

The Library of Congress catalogues this edition of this book as follows:

Purcell, Bernadette
Divorced As F• In Seven Spiritual Steps
Bernadette Purcell -1st ed.
TXu 2-276-105
Registration Date:
August 24, 2021
ISBN: 978-1-7378111-0-7 (hardcover)
ISBN: 978-1-7378111-1-4 (paperback)
ISBN: 978-1-7378111-2-1 (audio)

For Anica and Maylin
May the light be in you, with you, and as you.

For Beaner
May the light be all around you.

PREFACE

My very good friend Ellie's hairdresser's friend was also going through a divorce. When I asked the specifics of how she was getting through it, Ellie could not provide many details. I probed anyway because probing comes naturally to seasoned psychotherapists. I told Ellie that there was so much that this woman could be doing to grow from the experience. I wanted to be this woman's friend, therapist, and acquaintance, at the same time. I wanted to do all of these things without incurring a severe therapeutic conflict of interest, and also not seem like an obsessed stalker. This was proving to be quite difficult being that I did not know her name, nor did I live remotely close to her best friend the hairdresser, thereby assuming I also did not live close to her.

The resounding question stuck with me like a barnacle. How could I reach her? I had so many years of therapeutic acumen guiding me through my divorce. How could I tell her about it without actually being her therapist? I had such a strong support team helping me through incredibly tough times, how could I be part of her support team? How could I show her the skills that I developed through many years of helping others through their emotional upheavals, and deliver them like google maps for her stormy road ahead?

The answer seemed so simple. I would buy a book on divorce and give it to Ellie, to give to her hairdresser, who would pass it along to her friend. That seemed only slightly weird and stalkerish, but in a palatably unassuming way. As I walked the isles of the bookstore and breathed in one of my favorite scents in this entire world, I knew I was on to something. Books! I loved the feel of them, the sound of the page turning, and that smell! The experience of the store was life affirming, but the details were killing me. Every book I pulled off the shelf seemed ok, but not perfect. I wanted it to be more than a manual, less than a novel, and piercingly engaging. More than anything I wanted it to be funny while upholding the gravity of a heavy subject. I simply could not find it.

I walked out of that bookstore literally saying out loud, "Fuck, I have to write this fucker."

So, I set out to write a book that will guide, honor, love, entertain, and most importantly uplift its reader. This book is for Ellie and her hairdresser, while they so compassionately talk about how to help their friends going through similar life events, and to all friends who watch out for each other in their times of need. This book is a tool for those conversations about anyone going through difficult life events. It is a gift for a friend when words aren't enough, and a touchstone for the reader who doesn't know how much he or she needs it. But most directly, Ellie's hairdresser's friend, this book is for you.

CONTENTS

INTRODUCTION

IN VINO VERITAS

"Show me a sign!" Yes, I said it along with billions before me. "None of this veiled confusing bullshit. I haven't slept in days and I am not functioning at my highest capacity, so fucking hell, dumb it down for me and please make it clear. Neon lights will suffice. Thank you, and have a great day."

Was I talking to God? Probably. Was I talking to my inner self? Without a doubt, but most likely to both. My prayer was not particularly unique. God had heard this one before.

The sign I needed was a big glowing arrow at the fork in the road of life. Did I need to put all of my energy into wrangling back the person who just ended our marriage, or did I need to let him go, thereby starting the healing process? I had the will to do either. I had already been sharpening my lasso skills and roping him back into my circle with all of my might. Graveling was certainly not above me. But this was the point that I felt my reserves running thin. I needed to choose a direction and choose it wisely so that I didn't lose whatever I had left of my sanity.

What I needed from God was her take on where to put my energy. Did she want me to release him, or clutch on to him and insist that I was right and that his place was home with me? Release or cling. Your turn God. Go.

This pinnacle moment of transformation began while I was lying face down on the living room floor. The blanket of snow outside electrified the late morning light coming in from

1

the windows. As I lifted my head from the carpet to wipe my damp cheeks, I realized the wetness was an indecipherable combination of drool and tears. The carpet felt both harsh and soft, prickly yet safe. I was days past the blast of matrimonial separation, and the only clarity I had was the immediate processing of my senses. One hand drying the tear/drool combination, the other clutching the remote to a malfunctioning TV that I didn't know how to fix. I knew that my time on my cozy floor was limited because my children would certainly need my attention within minutes. The smell of Frosted Flakes would lead them to me, and I needed something better than a Tony the Tiger crime scene for them to walk into. My decision to start talking out loud was both my low and my high point.

I promised with all my might that I would be open to receive whatever sign she was capable of giving. My fingers were interlocked, as if that gave my words more of a direct line to God, and elbows were on the carpet. I brought myself first to army position, then all fours, and then almost standing. God was going to give me a sign and she was not going to give it to me while balancing myself on my coffee table. I used all of my conviction, stood up straight, and yelled up the stairs "Kids, hop in the car. We are going to see the rabbi."

My children understood this sentence much differently than most people. We are not Jewish and never have been, but my friend Rachel is the most amazing rabbi I have ever known. She breaks barriers with her big blond hair, bubbly personality, and beautiful smile to match. My kids knew her for how much they loved her children, and I knew her for how much I loved her. And on that day I needed a friend—a friend whose children would occupy my children and whose porous soapstone countertops would absorb my tears.

After a two-hour car ride, we pulled up to her oasis of a home. The long driveway, canopied by tall oaks and windchimes, brought us to her earthy door. As Rachel greeted my children, I unloaded my figurative and literal three pieces of baggage into her stone foyer. I stood tall until my kids ran off with her kids. For my collapse, I strategically angled my falling body onto her bar stools in a subliminal call for alcohol.

Ellie, my best friend who had seen me through every peak and valley since high school, was sitting on a bar stool next to me. For two and a half decades, she had been there for me, wearing the most stylish trends and hippest attitude to go with them. She chose to be an attorney, but could have been a Vogue stylist in a heartbeat. She had always been the singular reason I wore something other than athleisure clothing. This time, instead of greeting me with ways I could accessorize my outfit, she and Rachel greeted me with compassion in their eyes and mirrored shock in their hearts. We got together with nothing and everything to say as girlfriends often do.

Shoulders ladies, shoulders. That was all I really needed. Sweet shoulders to cry on and lament over my sadness and confusion. But fuck, that is not what my outspoken, extroverted, friends from my native Long Island gave me.

First order of operations was chardonnay.

"I don't know," I said, "I am already having such a hard time and I'm afraid a glass of wine will just make me a mess."

"Oh sweetheart," Rachel said in the most loving and condescending way. "You are already a complete mess whether you have this glass of wine or not, but we need to remove some daggers from your heart and wine will help us do that."

A few sips in and the Ghosts appeared. The first one came from somewhere deep inside Ellie as she gave me relentless accounts of my marriage as it was. She had officially become The Ghost of Relationship Past. She particularly had a very close view of my life. She and her husband had been coming to visit my ex and I for full weekends at a time. Every

Fourth of July weekend, we felt the same sandy heat, and cooled off with an iconic Jersey Shore BBQ. We were two very different couples finding commonality as we tasted the crunch of salty Jersey corn. Over a decade of beach weekends led to knowing the cadence of the other couple. I knew Ellie always made sure her husband had guy time. She could always count on him to watch the kids in the morning so she could exercise. They both watched over the other's dietary needs in a way that was so intimate and an obvious knowing of a person.

As a beach weekend eyewitness to everything, Ellie had many observations of her own. She came, she saw, and she burned it into her memory to be brought up during a time that I needed it most. And it turns out, the time that I most needed a hard hitting dose of reality was when I was crying into my goblet of wine about how unbelievable it was for a relationship so solid to end so abruptly.

As a side note, I will take this opportunity to add that this is certainly not my place to list the reasons for my divorce or his reasons for leaving. The one thing I know for sure is that you will never get an unbiased version from me. I only have my perspective, and that perspective has been reinforced by the many people who love me, and it is simply not a fair and balanced account of what actually happened. My ex-husband is quite accomplished at his job, but that job does not include writing in any way. He does not have the platform that I do to tell his story and it would disrespect what we had to give only my account of the end and not his. I will say he had his reasons to end it. We both put so much effort into trying to make the marriage work that we were spinning in confusion and tears and exhaustion. He tried. I tried. I loved him with such intensity that I would not have seen the end in front of me if it hit me like a wrecking ball. Which it did.

But I digress.

When I said she hit hard, I meant it. She tore apart the scenes that she had seen from my past with the vengeance of an ax murderer, and the precision of a surgeon. She zeroed in most pointedly on those moments that she would hear me complain about on the phone, and then came to my house and saw it with her own eyes.

"It was not ok, Bernie."

And there you go. That is the only quote I can pass along from Ellie because the rest would go into the territory of my perspective versus his. She did what a best friend would do with the information that she saw from her perspective. But what transposed her from being a friend to a maniacal apparition from my past was her relentless honesty. Every time I tried to soften the blow with circumstantial buffering, she would turn back and hit harder with truth blasts that zapped me out of my state of denial. "Wake the fuck up Bern, things weren't perfect! You were carrying so much weight for so long that you got used to the drag."

In vino veritas mother fuckers, the Ghost of Relationship Past was not going to let me have rose-tinted hindsight glasses.

I heard all that she had to say, and she was one wordy badass woman. Round after round of shots pointed at my marriage and I was still sitting there when the smoke cleared. Have you ever argued with a best friend who is also a lawyer, also an apparition, and also right? I don't advise it. I came up with the best response in my head, and then swallowed it along with my next sip of wine. I couldn't disagree with anything she was saying, as hard as it was to hear. Ellie saw the look of petrified shock on my face and put her arm around me while simultaneously filling my goblet with more chardonnay.

"My point is," she continued, "this is the part you can leave behind. You don't have to carry that weight around with you anymore."

I couldn't quite absorb it all, but I could hear it. I leaned my head on her shoulder as Rachel walked over to join in on the embrace.

"Plus," Rachel added, "you get to fall in love again."

"What?" I said feeling like the needle had just dragged across the record.

Que the Ghost of Relationship Future. Her talk of love felt preposterous at best, but I listened anyway. She was substantially less specific, and focused on easing my mind with positivity. She assured me with baller confidence that not only would I have a relationship in my future, but that it will be so much better because it would be free of all the bullshit brought up by her ghost of a counterpart. The aspect I liked most about her angle was that it was universal. Any relationship that ends is dysfunctional. Period, the end. The relationship ended and therefore had clearly expired. She honed in on the differences that exist between a functional relationship and a dysfunctional one.

I will list out these differences here because, my dear readers, they go for you too.

1. If you put even a fraction of the amount of effort into your next relationship as you did with this dysfunctional one, you will be shocked at the return.
    It turns out this is a thing. Dysfunctional relationships are like a bottomless pit. Trying to make them work feels like swimming against a rip tide. You dig your cupped hands into the water deeper and harder, but the current is too strong. After years of effort, you are deathly tired and even further away from shore.
2. "The next person will think you are a Goddess." She said this with complete sincerity. "You have so much to give and you have been giving it to the wrong person. There is nothing more tragic than efforts unseen and gifts left unopened. The next person will see you."

3. "The next person is so lucky because he gets the stronger you. You will come out of this stronger than ever and you will share that strength during the next leg of your journey."

4. When I asked how I could ever trust again, she didn't skip a beat and said, "Because that's who YOU are. You are a loving, trusting, caring person, and trusting again is part of the composite that makes you complete."

5. "I know you are not ready for this, but when you are there are so many people who I could set you up with!"

She was right. I was by no means ready, and I wouldn't be for a solid four months. But she made sure to leave that door open. She was, after all, the Ghost of Relationship Future, and it was her way to show this glimpse into the future came equipped with actual match-making skills like the Jewish mother I never had.

That night, with all the kids sleeping in the basement, I lay awake in a surprisingly comfortable dinosaur bed. I thought it was going to be just another sleepless night as I had had so many times by this point. Not sleeping had become my new normal, so instead of yearning for sleep, I just yearned for the soothing sound of a soul filled podcast. But this was not just any sleepless night. This one was torpedoed by the Ghost of Relationship Present. This ghost was nameless, faceless, and extremely succinct. This ghost came into my head in the form of God, or my inner being, or whoever the fuck I prayed to earlier that day, and delivered a five word message that sticks with me always. "He's doing you a favor." That was all this particular ghost had to say.

My usual position on such a blatant message in times past would have been to argue with it. How in holy hell could this blazing car bomb of a situation be interpreted as a favor? On what planet could betrayal be misconstrued as a gift? But by this point in my spiritual journey, I had learned to quiet those shouty thoughts as merely judgments that were doing me no good. In the quietude that followed, I let the words replay in my mind, and in their subtext became the deepest lesson of the night. "There are aspects of this journey that you cannot see right now, so just be thankful that you are on this road. It is one of enlightenment and rebirth. He is doing you a favor because this is the road you are SUPPOSED to be on." When Eckhart Tolle says, "Life will give you whatever experience is most helpful for the evolution of your consciousness," it pertains to situations like this. This was the moment I needed to wake the fuck up! The resistance I was feeling was that I did not want to wake the fuck up. I wanted to stay cozy and warm and in love with my husband. But instead, this whisper taught me to stop resisting reality.

As previously stated, I promised to be receptive of any sign that was thrown my way. I preferred for that sign to be in technicolor, but I was willing to settle for one that came to me in the form of a loud, temporarily schizophrenic voice in my head, calling the situation out for what it was, while comfortably resting in a dinosaur bed. The roar was evident and the recipient was willing. From this point onward, I had no choice but to acknowledge that this situation was my path. I deserved to take this bloodbath of divorce as the deepest lesson of my life, and my children deserved to garnish every benefit of that growth. If I missed this opportunity to benefit from this circumstance, then too much would be lost. Basically, if my children had to suffer the inconvenience of split holidays, then at least they could benefit from a fully actualized mother willing to impart this wisdom on their everyday lives.

The scariest part about dropping to the floor and praying to God for a sign was that she sent it, and because I promised to be receptive, I saw it. I saw it so clearly that my life became divided between the space of time before the auditory hallucination, and after it. Not only did she provide the sign, but she provided the precursor to the sign so that I would be able to understand it. My two ghosts had put me in the right head-space. With my past tribulations fresh on my mind, and my future hopefulness solidly in check, those five words came into my consciousness with complete understanding. I was not only receptive, I was comprehensive. I didn't need to think about the words, I needed to feel them. Absorb them to the depths of my core and keep them there as part of my personal make-up. I may have been extremely mad at him for his decision to leave, but I could no longer deny that he set a course that would ultimately make my life, and the lives of my children, better. In answering my question, God was quite clear. This was the moment I realized that I would come through this owning the fuck out of my divorce and teaching others to do the same. The seven spiritual steps came as they needed to, one at a time, and are detailed in the pages that follow.

AND NOW

So now what? You have decided, dear reader, to rise from your crouched position and take on the tall order of post-marital fuckery. A congratulations is in order because this is the exact place you need to be. In your life, in your day, and in your mind. Take a deep breath as I whisper in your ear, "You've got this." It may not feel like that all the time, but if you can read this sentence, if you can crack open this book, then there is no doubt that you can come out the other side of this dumpster fire of a situation feeling like you are actually glad for it all. Not necessarily glad that you had to go through it, but glad because you came out the other side of it a much more evolved, in-charge, better version of yourself. You will benefit from these changes, as will everyone around you. Your relationships, your work, your drive, and your life will burn brighter than it ever has before.

I know this because of all the activities you could be doing right now, you chose to read a book. And of all the books you could have chosen, you chose this one. There is a deep and profound reason for that, and it will reveal itself in time. But for now, know that the lessons I have imparted from having gone through this, combined with my experience as a psychotherapist, will guide you in a needed direction. This is a crossroad. Many people have veered toward instability and negativity at this juncture. By going on this journey with me, you are setting yourself up to take the other path. One that will lead you to an unbelievable lightness. The only thing I am asking for in return is that you trust in me, in these words, and in the direction I am going to lead you. Your inner strength is already there, but you are sitting in a place of extreme emotion. Emotions have a tendency to wreak havoc on even the strongest of warriors. I am going to teach you to harness these emotions in a way that will help you to feel whole and complete again.

As you walk through this journey, you will learn to take every situation with strong resolution and preparedness. Ultimately, you will go through your divorce like someone who has been there before. It will feel more like a second time passing through these particular circumstances because each step will feel like you have been prepared. You will dial in and walk through it like a champion racecar driver doing an extra lap after she has earned her gold cup. You know these streets, you will walk this path, and it will all feel like a deja vu. I have blazed this path for you and I have done it from a place of awareness. Each path is unique, but there are certain lessons that are universally beneficial.

This lesson, this wisdom, is yours for the taking. That by no means makes it easy. This is a difficult uphill climb and you will feel the steepness of it at every turn. But when done right, the destination becomes envious of the journey, and you become the recipient of every gem picked up along the way. These gems, or nuggets of wisdom, will be yours to use over and over again during your times of sorrow, rebirth, enlightenment, silliness, frustration, and triumph. My darling, let's begin.

CHAPTER ONE

GATHER YOUR RESOURCES

Point Guard

In the weeks following ground zero, I heard an overwhelming amount of advice from everyone I encountered. All of which was said with love and best intentions, but very difficult to sift while trying to make it through life hour by hour. The one piece of resounding advice that I just could not ignore was "Get yourself a lawyer," and it played on my mind like an annoying television jingle. I did not want a lawyer. I wanted my husband and I to work through the end of our marriage just as we had the beginning—together. I simply could not fathom making decisions with a person other than the person who had been my partner for 12 years.

Who did I trust? That was the hardest question for me to answer. My heart told me to continue to trust the husband who had my back in countless ways for so long. My gut told me to find someone neutral to take the reins. Every divorce is so personal and so specific, so I can't speak for everyone here, but when emotions are high, the decision making process is highly compromised. This was compounded by the fact that I was not sleeping, not eating, and very fearful. How did I make a decision during that time? I didn't. Instead, I just listened.

I listened to the same advice given to me by every friend, every family member, every colleague, and even my hair dresser: "Get yourself a lawyer."

The fear that I found in getting a lawyer was the charges. I am perfectly ok with paying for a job well done, but what about the upcharges? What about the game lawyers are known to play by saying you need to be way more aggressive than you actually need to be just so they can reap the benefits of the upcharge. Scary. Does it happen? Yes. You need to be careful. But lawyers are similar to other professions in that they rely on personal recommendations. If they want you to recommend them to all of your divorcing friends, then they will want to be as fair as possible. Overall, you need to build a team. For many, a lawyer is a strong part of that team because he or she will go about every decision with a rational, clear head. Objectivity is a necessary tool, and a lawyer has that, plus years of experience dealing with the details of divorce.

Not only was I swimming through a sea of "you need a lawyer right now" advice, I was also aware that I couldn't just go with the first one I found. I needed to interview them and shop around a bit before finding the right fit. But how could I do this with my diminished mental capacity and obliterated sense of trust? How could I begin the process of dissolving the marriage that I wanted most in this world to keep together? I was finding it very difficult to conduct interviews for a lawyer because I simply did not want one. I did not want a divorce. I did not want any part of the process, but I was acutely aware that this train had already left the station. If I was going to release him, this was an important part of that process. The divorce was happening and I needed to make a move before I found myself exposed and unprotected.

With the next step illuminated, I dusted the cobwebs off my power pantsuit and got dressed one foot at a time. I arrived a half hour early for my first meeting with a lawyer and sat in my car frozen. I turned off the ignition but couldn't open the car door. My body turned into a stubborn pile of dead weight and refused to move.

My resistance was kept at bay all that morning as I got ready for the free consultation, but sitting in that parking lot brought a surge of "the whys" with unrelenting abandon. Why am I here? Why is this happening? Why is it so cold out? I took a moment to gather my energy and refocus. After all, it's just a conversation with a person who is on my side... right?

I opened my designer bag and reviewed my diligently prepared questions as my body began to loosen up. I had everything I needed to begin an informed discussion on the breakdown of my marriage. I found some motivation to move from my SUV as the heat dissipated into the frosty air. Before heading into the warm waiting room, I decided that it would be great to have something to look forward to after the meeting.

"Want to meet up for coffee later?" The question seemed simple enough.

I picked up the phone. I called my sister Faith. In walked the point guard.

She answered the phone and said the expected and friendly, "Hey."

The words "want to meet up later?" simply escaped me. As did all other words. It was like all languages everywhere just vanished, leaving me with nothing but my foggy breath. I tried to squeeze out even just a noise, but my vocals chords were frozen. I felt the air just not going into my lungs and the world started spinning.

And then I heard her voice on the line. "It's ok, just take your time. I am going to be here listening whenever you are ready to speak." Then silence.

I felt my lungs fill with air. I took the time to simply catch my breath. She sat there silently.

Finally, the prophetic words came to me, but "um" was all I could get out. She once again said, "I'm here."

I took a few more moments. With all the strength I had in my body I said, "Can we meet up later? I'm having a really tough day."

"Name the time and place," was her reply.

I have no idea how she knew to do that. She intuitively knew that the silence on the line was not a faulty connection or an erroneous mute button. It was her sister in a tremendous amount of pain and completely terrified to take one step closer to a divorce lawyer's office. She knew that I did not need platitudes or words of encouragement. What I needed was her presence. Her attentive, kind, patient presence. Slowly I found my breath; and with my breath I found my voice. During this time, I had one sister to help me repair my head, and another sister to help me repair my heart. It was like they both shadowed the other in a never-ending ring of support. Through the ugly, murky, thick of it all, Faith and Kai became my go-to. Faith had this combination of intelligence, intuition, and even possibly a touch of ESP. Her advice was always on point and it helped me to streamline the chaotic mess that was in my brain. For this reason and so many more, Faith became my point guard, or that is to say she became my coach on the field of divorce. Kai had been a trailblazer in my life since birth. As the older sister, she learned to go through life's obstacles, break them down for me, and tell me what to expect. I can say with certainty I do not know how I would have managed without the proverbial harbinger of life's tribulations without sis Kai. She got married two years before me, had two kids two years before me, and got divorced two years before me. How could I not take advantage of that dynamic treasure trove of life experience?

Not everyone has a Kai or Faith in his or her life. I am well aware of that. But you do have people you can call. In addition to calling people, this is a perfect time to join things. Join a kickball league, join a religious service, join a book club, or ask your coworkers to go to happy hour. Expanding your network will help you in limitless ways, and there has never been a better time to sharpen those networking skills. As your network grows and you begin to meet people, you will find that most people have been through a breakup of some kind. They know the pain of it and want to be there for you. Let them.

This spiritual step is called "gather your resources," but I just as easily could have called it "pick up the phone." That is your primary step in creating a solid foundation. You need to pick up the phone and use it to reach out to people for help. Call your people that you know are there for you. Call a lawyer and begin your interviews. Call your therapist and double down on your sessions. If you don't already have a therapist, please get one immediately. Just keep calling. The people who will be best for your healing process will emerge.

I am a mental health therapist and have been in practice for well over a decade. I utilize the advice and lessons learned from my practice in all that I do. I often tell my patients to gather their resources for various situations. There are times in your life when you just have to recognize that your chips are down. Life has thrown you a curveball that would be difficult for anyone to handle. As you are gathering your resources, keep in mind that humans are social creatures, and when they see a person in need, they will make an effort to rise to the occasion. Not everyone knows exactly how to respond, so allow them the chance to fumble, as long as you are allowing them to help in whatever capacity they know how.

It also helps to diversify your calls. Know the person who is there for a laugh, the one who will take you up on a walk, and the one who will sit there as you cry. Local support groups are also extremely plentiful. There is a support group for every malady and there has never been more ways to connect with them than now. When you are in the middle of emotional distress, it is imperative that you understand that there are people out there wanting and waiting for your call. As Mr. Rogers once said, "When I was a boy and I would see scary things in the news, my mother would say to me, 'Look for the helpers. You will always find people who are helping.'" Scary things will happen. When you are faced with a scary thing, look for the people who are there to help you. Learn to recognize how to let them help you. As a therapist, I can say this with absolute sincerity. I went into this profession because I want to help you. There is a therapist near you right now, waiting.

When I called Faith, I didn't know how much I needed a strong supportive voice until I heard it. The reason for the call did not emerge until after I made it. The reasons for your calls will reveal themselves when they need to. All the players on the field will take their places and gather as the formidable team that you need for your foundation of strength.

OH WAIT, AM I ON A DATE?

As I look around the room, I discover that I am right smack in the middle of a scene somewhere between a romance novel and a "Twin Peaks" experience.

There was a glass of wine in my hand, a roaring fire, and a handsome man returning from the kitchen with cheese and crackers that my anxiety-ridden stomach would never tolerate.

This moment randomly coalesced by taking the only actionable advice given to me by the divorce lawyer from only a few days prior. "Become familiar with the real estate in your area," he said during our foggy conversation. After speaking on the phone with Faith, I gathered my strength and marched into my first meeting with a lawyer. The rest of his advice about finances and family court had no real sticking power, but real estate seemed more grippy and forward thinking. So, my confused, sleep deprived and malnourished brain decided to dial in on only the real estate part of the meeting.

House hunting seemed like the obvious next step for single women. As I swiped through the app version of "Real Estate for Dummies," I came across a neighborhood that I had admired for years. Great school system, beautiful homes, tree lined sidewalks, and the vaguely familiar essence of an ex-boyfriend. Only a small 18 years had passed since I helped an ex named Ben move into one of these houses. The memory of boxes and the excitement on his face as we walked through his new empty living room came rushing back to me. I had such vivid imagery of him speaking of turning the house into his dream home that I could almost touch the wall markings and smell the freshly cut wood. The funny thing about memories is they don't care or even notice the passing of 18 years. What was yesterday is today in the mind's eye. What happened next was because of the confluence of curiosity and newly single liberation. I typed his name into the Facebook search bar because... why the fuck not? Also, I needed to take my own advice to reach out to people, and I saw no reason to leave old flames out of that list. So yes, like a beacon of social media joy, Ben's face came smiling back at me from a photo of him standing right in front of that same house that I remembered.

My direct message on Facebook went something like, "Hey there, I have a very random question for you. I have been seriously thinking of moving to !@#$, and I assume you still live there. Any advice on places I should look for or avoid? Any local knowledge you have would help so much. I hope you are well. Cheers." It was vague but also friendly, which was the exact look I was going for.

Not only did he have advice, he hopped right on to the hunt for my information. Within a few short exchanges, we established that we were both single and happy to be back in contact again. I forgot how good men are at figuring out a single woman with precision and veiled eagerness. He said that house hunting was his "thing" and offered to join my house hunting expedition throughout his town. This was perfect because it meant that not only did I not have to carry out my lawyer's advice alone, but I could catch up with a person from my past while drinking up tons of local real estate knowledge.

The next day as I pulled up to his house to start the Zillow Adventure, I was surprised at how different his house looked. Same long driveway, but the trees on either side of it went from saplings to fully grown, and the vines on the porch signified years of attention to detail. I was glad when he came to my car to greet me because, although I knew him at one time, he was at that point a stranger. Walking into a

21

stranger's house was a step into the unknown that I was not willing to take. However, the step out of my car to greet his perfectly familiar face was a joy to take. We hugged in that ex-lover type of way. It was an embrace that was both rusty and smooth; familiar and foreign.

Ben held me by the shoulders to take that extra look, smiled, and said that he was so happy to see me. He looked striking in that breath of fresh air type of way. Like my past was reaching up from the cosmos telling me that certain things never change. I will always be a sucker for brown eyes and a scruffy beard.

The day was true to form. We toured many houses, townhomes, and condos. Since my lawyer's advice was to "familiarize," I didn't have any significant agenda. Throughout the day, he pointed out the best attributes of his town with the knowledge of an art gallery tour guide and the enthusiasm of a puppy.

"Look here," he pointed out. "You could fix this area up as a playroom for your girls." And then later, "Next we should check out the town center. There's a ton of cool spots to see there." I was dazzled by the town and beautiful homes and eating it all up.

I was so filled with gratitude that he would spend his Sunday touring houses with me that I felt like an end of day toast was in order. The truth was I didn't want the day to end, but since the Zillow tour was over, I didn't know how to extend it. Nor did I know anything about the freedom that was so recently bestowed upon me. How do two people who are not married continue on to the next activity? The words came out clumsily sounding something like, "What a great day! Can I take you out for a drink as a thank you?"

He laughed. "No," he said while trying to contain the rest of his laughter, "but I have a great bottle of Chianti waiting for us back at the house." Damn this guy was good.

I wasn't sure why my invitation caused laughter. Was I that out of the game? Yes, but I didn't care. Also, by this point he was solidly not a stranger. He was back to being Ben. The same guy that I worked with at my first post-college job. The same guy who convinced me to go to grad school out of sheer love of learning. And the same guy who was never a match enough for the relationship to ever take wings. Over the course of a few hours, he jumped right out of his Facebook pics and into himself. The one who I knew and maybe, at one point, even loved. Now don't get too excited. Ben was not the man you would want me to end up with. We broke up 18 years prior for good reason and those reasons still existed. Which was why I continued to think that this was still not a date. Just two people catching up over a love of open houses and good wine.

We pulled up to his home that held the span of time that separated us. Those walls saw his marriage begin and end. They saw his elation, his disappointment, and his moving on. They saw me return to the space as a different person, some-how more confident but equally unsure of the future. As we went inside, I tried to place the memories with the actual in-terior of the home, but nothing fit. Our relationship was not a witness to the house in its functioning form. We broke up well before the furniture arrived. The wood paneling was gone, and was replaced by Benjamin Moore moody gray and wainscoting. The kitchen was facing a different direction and had perfectly placed items from Homegoods strewn about, but were never actually used. It was the kitchen of a bachelor that looks pretty but collects dust out of neglect. He never mounted a television in the place that he once dreamed he would, but he did fix up the wood burning fireplace.

He got to work right away. He lit the fire like a boy scout and poured two glasses of wine. As he handed me my glass, he pointed to a photo album on his coffee table. It was the old fashioned type with actual printed photos that were never intended to gain likes on social media. Just organic old photos of smiling people beginning their journey of adulthood. Our relationship was not long enough to fill up the entire album, but it was long enough to make an impression. There we were, hand in hand in front of the Epcot globe, wearing tourist sneakers and comfortable jean shorts.

As he returned to the kitchen for the cheese plate, I stared at the photo while letting the moment catch up with me. I felt that feeling that happens seconds after hopping off a treadmill and your pace suddenly feels too fast. I looked down at my glass of wine as I kneeled in front of the coffee table. The scene was innocent enough, just two people catching up, but it somehow turned into date territory. Was it the fire, the wine, or the privacy of his house that turned it into a date? I couldn't tell, but it was a scene that never would have been ok only one month prior. The very act of getting in touch with an old flame would never have happened in my old life. The freedom felt unearned and out of place, but it was mine for the taking.

I knew nothing of the single scene, or dating, or even if I was on one, but I knew how to live up the moment. I was the arbiter of my surroundings that I let happen piece by piece. My bruised ego didn't need to hear the compliments that followed, but I let them happen too.

"You have always been the one that got away. I kicked myself for so long for letting that happen."

Why did that sound so good coming from a man with whom I had no intentions of starting a relationship? My bruised ego drank it up like a dehydrated sponge. It gave me the feeling of being wanted again which was lightyears better than feeling used up and discarded. Every word from his mouth helped me sit just a bit taller. One sentence per vertebrate, and after a full conversation my confidence and my posture was fully replenished.

I felt like thanking him for restoring that piece of myself and for being so perfectly timed. I wanted that feeling of moving on with a new and different person, but only in a situation that felt safe. Having already known him, he was the perfect combination of new and safe. He was exciting but also trusted. Instead of thanking him for super charging my ego, I thanked him for the wine, and for the day and for the hours of great conversation.

On the ride home, I could feel the inflated sense of self. *Absolutely*, I thought. *Please wine and dine me and help me feel valued again! Connect my worth to the delicious compliments from a man and I can feel whole once more. Yummy compliment sprinkles poured all over this ego boost ice cream sundae.* I devoured it all ravenously and woke up the next morning looking for more.

As the thoughts circled around in my head and provided the much needed mood enhancing cocktail, I looked for ways to keep it going. How could I elongate the high provided by another person? Searching, processing, needing more became both addicting and exhausting. While lost in thought and trying needlessly to search for something outside of myself, I realized I was once again giving away my power. If my mood was contingent on the compliments from Ben, how could I maintain the high? I was putting my sense of value in the hands of another person, and that needed a swift and abrupt change. So I pivoted. Quite possibly the most impactful, delectable, sweetest pivot of my life. So let me explain.

I clearly needed a serious talking to from none other than my inner self. One could say that this inner dialogue was still the Ghost of Relationship Present, or God, or the angels that guide me throughout my life. All of this could have been true, but I just didn't feel profound enough to include divine or otherwise intervention on this one. This just sounded like Bernie, and my opinion of myself was high enough to sometimes go with the wisdom that my 40 years provided. During my self-rant, I spelled it out in layman's terms that even my raw parts could understand. When I use all my esoteric therapist mumbo jumbo on myself, I tend to get confused, and it results in me running away from honesty. So I kept it short and swallowed the simple, palatable message.

"This is temporary Bern. Not only do you not need an ego boost, you don't need your ego. You can be free of the yearnings of the ego and create space for your glorious, unbridled, inner self to exist. And the best part, it is not contingent on the temporary musings of others, because it is already within you. You do not need the man from last night, and you certainly do not need the man who left you after 10 years of marriage. You may feel like an abandoned pile of dog shit now, but you were not abandoned, and you are not dog shit. However, you can use that feeling to strip yourself of all attachments and rise up stronger than you have ever been. You will benefit so much from this, your children will benefit so much from this as they absorb all that their inspired mother provides."

The sweet beautiful pivot changed my trajectory from seeking to owning. I didn't need to search for something that was already inside of me. All I needed to do was step aside and let it all unfold.

TRAVELING WISE WOMEN

I spent a good amount of time making calls and gathering resources. I called local friends and distant ones. I contacted neighbors and set up emergency arrangements. I joined a divorce support group and knew that I might actually make it to one of their meetings one day. I reached out in so many ways knowing that a portion of it was likely to stick. Solo parenting offers new challenges that need forethought. I could no longer rely on the divide and conquer method. I called other parents and offered to carpool, babysit, stop by in a pinch, and vice versa. Making those calls was a low energy way to secure a feeling of safety.

With my team securely in place it was time to start strategizing. There were so many things that needed to be done and I had no idea what the timeline should look like. I had already familiarized myself with real estate in the neighborhoods of ex-boyfriends, but was selling my house really the right move? If so, where would I go? Could I afford the district I was living in? How would I know what I could afford? Every question brought on an avalanche of more questions, and I needed someone who was feeling slightly less stressed and emotional to help me answer them. It turns out, the worst time to strategize a new chapter in your life is when you are still reeling from the last one. I had no idea where to begin, and since I was still in a mental place where finishing a bowl of soup was an extremely difficult task, I knew reinforcements were necessary.

I knew how to take my own advice as I had done so many times before. I could tell that my reserves were once again running thin and that I couldn't handle it all on my own. I needed for my children to be occupied so that I could plan out the next stage in my life. Although I had many occasions of calling on my resources by this point, on this day I didn't know if I made a call to anyone. I just opened the front door and in walked my support team. Like a feminine version of the biblical trio, my three wise women followed the North Star of Divorce and wound up at my doorstep. My mother came with two fistfuls of diet coke, one for herself and one to share, Faith came with aromatherapy room spray, and Kai came with her two children to play with mine (the best gift for any parent). It was the post break-up version of gold, frankincense and myrrh.

With my children occupied elsewhere, the room smelling like soothing lavender, and our glasses fogging up with cold diet coke, we were ready for the pow wow of the century. I was so touched and honored that they made their way through the wintery cold to help me with my unending life strategy questions. But before I could begin to ask, they took one look at me and said, "You should go take a nap."

"But I don't want a nap!" I said like a toddler. "I want to be here with you guys. Are you for real?"

Just like during an Irish goodbye, it is considered polite to not burden your host with your own departure; in my Irish family, it is considered an honor to show up somewhere and take a nap. To arrive at someone's home, breeze past them and say, "I'll be right with you… right after a quick nap," means that you are considered family. In some backward way, the people you take for granted are only close family, so therefore the more you take someone for granted, the more you must consider them family. From this frame of reference, typical greetings in my family include "Feeling harried from a long drive? Go take a nap. Feeling a bit hungover from the holiday? Go take a nap. Kids had you up all night? Yep, definitely take a nap!"

I was used to this sentiment as a party goer, but as the party host it just didn't feel right. I told them of my consternation, but they still urged, "You clearly need it. Don't worry, we will watch your kids, it will be good for you to rest!"

"Guys, you don't get it. The thing I fear most right now is nighttime because it means I am supposed to sleep. It means I need to be alone with my thoughts in darkness. I have plenty of time for that every night and right now it's the last thing I need!" I really didn't think I would find myself graveling with my sisters to just let me hang out with them instead of sleeping in the middle of the afternoon, but nothing else was really making sense, so I wasn't exactly surprised. They had been there for five minutes and were already annoying me with their pushy demands to force me to relax. My weakened state left me with a very short fuse and I found myself getting annoyed very easily.

My mom broke up the adult version of sibling rivalry with the perfect gesture. She handed me a throw blanket and sat down next to me. She didn't say a word. She just sat there with the ice clinking in her glass and a shoulder to lean on. The unsaid portion of the afternoon was what we already knew. We all knew I hadn't slept in weeks. We all knew I had no idea what to tell them about the whys, or the next steps, or the big questions. Under normal circumstances, I would have known about the arrival of any guest, and probably had a perfectly-timed organic gluten free casserole coming out of the oven to greet them. But on this day, I had no idea if I had invited them or if they showed up; I had a fridge full of kid food, and no memory of the last time I had eaten.

They didn't mention any of that, but just looked at me with compassion. They sat down next to me in a sister circle and told me it was going to be ok. They forgave me for not napping and offered words of support. They said things like, "You're so strong, Bernie," and "You got this, girl." I sat in silence absorbing their words but shaking my head. I appreciated and needed their presence so much, but from my perspective, their words were a bunch of horseshit. I so strongly disagreed with what they were saying that I just couldn't let them go on.

"How could you possibly say that!" I said emphatically. "I am not strong at all! I am seriously breaking here." And then, like an unwanted tidal wave, the rush of pain came pouring out of me. It rose up from my heart and through my tear-soaked face. "I have never felt so lost and confused. It feels like I'm just going in circles, and..." I gasped to catch my breath as my hands covered my face, "I can't stop crying. I can barely hold myself up and I can't stop crying. I am such a mess!" I wanted them to stay in my home, but only so I could slam the door and tell them to leave me alone. I wanted to feel their support but also hide my fear, shame, and grief right along with me under the alpaca throw blanket.

"But don't you see," Faith said in a calm steady voice, "that is what strength is!" Her voice was so soothing and re-assuring. It almost put me to sleep, but in a good way. Faith continued, "I heard you on the phone today with your kids. You were helping them find their boots and taking them out in the snow. You made them lunch and made sure they felt your love in whatever way you could give it. You held yourself together all day, and then with the kids out of ear shot, you chose this moment surrounded by supportive women to let the pain come rushing out. THAT is strength! Trust me, my dear sister, you are so strong."

I took my hands away from my eyes and looked up. For the first time in a long time I believed her. It made sense to me and it cleared the path for the only thing I found to be truly important. As long as I could continue being their mother, as long as I could show them all the love that I knew how to give, I was heading in the right direction.

All the questions that I needed them to answer seemed to melt away. The question of where to move was for a different sleepless night and day. This day was all about doing the one thing that came naturally to me regardless of my state of mind. Taking care of my two little monsters was all I needed to focus on. Parenting is a constant paradox, especially during any familial upheaval. Children are a source of strength but also the complete depletion of it. During times of unrest, they need you more than ever; but that is also the time you want to crawl into a hole and lick your wounds. However, your focus, energy, and attention needs to be on them. According to the theory of 'fake it till you make it,' being strong for another person helps you to be strong for yourself. It helps you to channel your energy on only what is most important.

That is how kids give you strength. But then there are the moments, every parent has had thousands of them, when your child gives you so much strength your heart could burst. Like when Avery woke me up one morning and said, "Mama, it's so weird. I have had this song in my head ever since I dreamed about it last night, and now I can't stop singing it. Can we play it Mama?" Of course, I didn't want to disappoint my seven-year-old, so I ran groggily to the speakers in the bathroom (because, acoustics) and she played "Fight Song" by Rachel Platten! I can't quote the song because there are a ton of copyright laws about quoting music in literature, with good reason. Those words were not meant to be read but to be belted out at the top of your lungs. I urge you to give it a listen. It is probably the most empowering, soul filling, beautiful song I have ever heard. She and I danced around the bathroom singing at the top of our lungs. Her with her blond hair and effervescent smile, and me with my pajamas and messy ponytail sang the shit out of that song. I swear sometimes she has a knowing that goes so far beyond her age. I worked very hard at not showing her the pain I had inside, but she could detect it somehow. Her response was to give me the most uplifting gift in a way that a seven-year-old knows how to deliver. That is the embodiment of compassion. That is love.

Love is also the three traveling wise women who helped me to prioritize my heartbreak. Before I could go on to make big life decisions, I needed to know where my strength was. Emotional stress can shake a person's confidence, so knowing how to channel and recognize strength in its various forms becomes essential. What they showed me was that breaking down was part of being strong. My disparaging self talk was totally off point. It takes strength to let it out. Like a muscle that tears grows bigger and stronger, a person with a torn heart will grow bigger and stronger—especially when you have the presence of mind to let it come out during a time that it will be well received.

For those inopportune times, when the flood came unannounced and unwanted, there was always a small escape to the bathroom. I went to the bathroom to handle a rush of emotion so many times during those first few months post breakup that my children thought I had a potty issue. It was better for them to think that my issue was gastrointestinal than to think that there was something seriously wrong in my world. But on the rare occasion, when a tear or two would slip through the cracks, I would reassure them that adults get sad sometimes too, and that it is perfectly ok to cry. The overarching message I wanted to convey to my children was that I had it all under control. The best way for them to learn about human emotion was from a place of security. If their world was safe, they could stretch and grow in meaningful, small doses.

I looked up at my traveling wise women and knew I needed to let my new found resolve develop for a while. I was tired and it was getting late.

"Thanks so much for coming," I said to them. "I have a long road to go before I feel stable again. And an even longer road to go to feel happy. I think I will need to have those divorce papers in hand before I can feel truly happy again."

"NO!" Faith jumped in. For a woman so kind natured, she was sometimes shockingly aggressive. "Happiness is a state of being. You do not need anything outside of yourself to feel happy."

"Whoa! What the fuck, Faith? When did you become Buddha? You are dead on balls accurate and I will never say that again." I said it and I meant it.

It was like she dug her hand inside of my guts and pulled out the most freeing and enlightening concept. It was a concept that I already knew but was buried under insecurities and self doubt. Once she recovered it from deep inside of me and threw it in my face, I could not ignore the truth behind her words. Happiness is a state of being. You do not have to wait for the house to sell, for the new job to start, for your shift to end, or for anything really. Happiness is a choice and you make it every moment. Not all moments are meant to be happy, but you do not have to delay your happiness until the arrival of something better. You can find happiness during times of unrest. You can find peace during times of chaos. You can find stillness during times of uncertainty.

After a day of talking and crying and talking some more, my three lovely wise women went home. I had a lot to chew on from their visit. I knew I would continue to call on them for support and utilize what the universe had put in front of me. I wasn't afraid to admit that I needed help, and by reaching out, I showed people how to help me. When people would ask how they could help, I knew to be very specific. People don't know how to respond to vague ideas of future help, but they do know how to respond to, "I need a new yoga buddy," or, "Yes please, come over and order Chinese!" These are the simple things that combine practicality with human kindness.

I asked many different things of many different people. Part of my strength was calling on the strength of others. One of my biggest requests was to just be. Divorce can be very lonely. You no longer have the constant companionship of another adult. So my request to "just be" came out in the form of "let's hang."

Anything is better than isolating. Kai came over so many times I thought she might move in.

I have a tendency to get bizarrely interested in strange things for a short amount of time. It's like an ephemeral deep plunge into some odd curiosity that fades as quickly as it came in. I didn't realize that she was humoring me until she said one day, "Sure, I'll watch another documentary about serial killers" with a knowing smile. I realized she had no interest whatsoever in serial killers. She acutely knew that I needed her to "just be." In time, she would go back to being my friend/sister, but until then she was the person that helped me face life until I healed. A person to just be there, standing strong, as I pontificated the elusiveness of Ted Bundy.

ON THERAPY

"Do not believe that he who seeks to comfort you lives untroubled among the simple and quiet words that sometimes do you good. His life has much difficulty and sadness and remains far behind yours. Were it otherwise he would never have been able to find those words." Rainer Maria Rilke

I thank the universe every day for my resources; they are my friends and family and I couldn't imagine life without them. However, there are some resources for which one needs to pay. I love the term "lawyer up," and I also love the term "therapist up." I am clearly biased in any effort to persuade someone to see a therapist. One could say that since it's my profession, I could have a subconscious desire to legitimize and over value the benefits therein. But that would be putting the chicken before the egg, or the other way around; but either way it's backward. I went into this profession because of its legitimacy and value and knew that I was the perfect person for the job.

When I was in college as a wee young psychology major, I landed a job bartending at a little dive bar on Long Island called Captain Jacks. Anyone who grew up on Long Island knows that a love for Billy Joel and his localized lyrics are a prerequisite for a true Islander. And therefore, his song about "Captain Jack" was a much debated point at this particular bar located in the heart of Billy's hometown. "Which came first," someone would inevitably say, "the bar or the song?" The owners of course loved this debate and encouraged it whenever possible. Like any good dive bar, the first half of the shift was filled with post-work stressed out patrons who wanted to be anywhere but home, and later the bar filled with late night post party 20-somethings ready to forget the last portion of their night. The volume of patrons would crescendo like clockwork from a straggling few to a hopping bar three deep with bills in their hands.

Both of these portions of the bartending night brought me such joy, but it was in the first half of the shift that I experienced the budding use of my psychology 101 textbook knowledge. With just a few people sitting at my bar, and thousands of lemons and garnishes to cut in preparation for the onslaught of barely legal drinkers, I had time to really talk to the patrons while meticulously working the paring knife. The happy hour crowd, at least the ones who would sit at the bar, were generally stressed and in need of a stiff drink. I poured their alcohol, and they poured their hearts out to a therapist in training. Asking the right questions at the right time just came naturally to me. My compassion for their plight, combined with a genuine curiosity of the details that got them there, had them sitting on that bar stool for hours as the tips became proportionately larger. So not only did this job afford me the opportunity to really hear the stories of total strangers, but I was also being paid quite well to do it.

Years of undergrad went by fueled by the tips of extremely appreciative half-drunk people twice my age. They divulged and I listened. I also remembered every detail thanks to the help of copious notes that I hid behind the bar. In the form of flash cards (students are students), I would write one up for each patron. "Rick, 40ish, salt/pepper beard, Heineken until he switches to Knob Creek, wants to switch careers but doesn't know how." Rick always sat at the bar and put his wallet out in front of him where he could see it. He seemed to like being in sales but would get that dreamy eyed look whenever talking about his band. The tips of his fingers were callused from playing guitar and would give his passion away in a story only his body could tell. The stories of the patrons were easy to remember, but their names and drink choices would often trip me up, hence the need for the quick flash card check as they walked in the door. "Hey Rick, how about another Heineken?" I would say with a smile to the man of about 40 with a salt and pepper beard. And just like that, there was not another bar stool that could take the place of that one. His softened countenance showed just how valued, welcome, and remembered he seemed to have felt.

The draw to therapy as a profession was unmistakable. I studied at school during the day, and put my new found knowledge to use at night. It seemed natural and organic. I was aware that I needed an incredible amount more schooling and experience to open my practice doors; actually, it would take me the better part of a decade to "hang my sign" as a licensed therapist, but the process was enjoyable. I knew from the beginning that if hearing the stories of strangers felt natural while simultaneously making drinks, running the register, and chopping gallons of fruit, imagine what I could do with an actual office and proper training!

The journey of education for a therapist is never done. The newbies, with their freshly minted licenses and spanking new sofas offer an energy that is boundless and spirited. The therapists with a little more seasoning offer more experience and wisdom that contributes to the textbook knowledge. Most therapists will continue their education by adding trainings and certificates that are relevant to their practice. This keeps the therapist up to date on the current therapeutic trends as well as offers a path to specialization. When a therapist specializes in something, you can be pretty sure the road to that specialization was more experiential than textbook. It typically doesn't happen until years of practice and skills have been honed and personalized. Therapy is a subjective art because there are many ways to interpret what is said during each session. A good therapist will know how to hop into the space in which the client is living, which will guide rapport and build trust.

Many people have asked me how they can find a therapist and I often give the same advice. "Take a minute," I say to them. "Sit back and think about the demographic that would most suit you in your life right now. Do you want to be discussing things with someone much older? Younger? Your age? Does gender matter? What is important is to have an idea in your head about the demographic that will most serve you now."

"Once this is done, hop on to Google and get yourself a list of names in the area. A therapist also needs to be a savvy business person, and any professional should have a website. Go through a few websites and make a few calls. Don't talk to a secretary, only directly to the therapists themselves. If you feel relaxed and excited to begin work with the person you have chosen, then you are on the right path."

This stage in the process is so important because it takes a lot of energy to begin therapy. You want for that energy to circulate in the right place with the right person. Your time is worth it.

Joining this field as a professional felt like a no-brainer to me. Admitting to myself that I needed to sit on the other side of the couch took a bit more convincing. Especially because, and this goes for everyone, the time when you most need therapy is also the time when you are likely the most depleted and confused. For most people, the nudge to begin therapy might come from a friend, a family member, or even a surprisingly poignant book on divorce.

I nudged myself after giving birth to my first daughter. I was feeling the exhaustion that any new mother feels and I knew the demographic that would most serve me. I wanted a therapist who intrinsically understood the birth and pregnancy process without having to explain it. I wanted a female therapist at or older than childbearing age. I looked at a few websites and made a few calls just like I advised myself to do. I am good at both giving and receiving advice, especially when they are one in the same. I found a website that boasted "Find Your Balance." The therapist was a woman named Bettie and hit my optimal demographic in every way. Because she was a woman who already had two kids, I figured we could just skip over the whole "Wow becoming a parent is a fucking cyclone" conversation and just start somewhere closer to the middle. When I called her, there was something about her voice that seemed calming as well as directive, and that was the energy I needed. I set up an appointment and signed up for the ride.

First appointments can be difficult for the patient. This is not the case for the therapist, though; we love meeting you and finding out what makes you tick. Common first appointment phrases include, but are not limited to, "I don't even know where to start, my life is a mess, it just feels overwhelming, I don't even know if this is an issue," and other vague and highly generalized statements. It is then the therapist's job to help the patient specify what the problem really is, and best ways to cope, manage, and work through it. Basically, if conversation were a ship, the patient is the one at the helm, turning and adjusting speed when necessary, while the therapist is the ocean underneath, helping to provide currents that steer the patient toward a calm understanding and closure at the end of the 50 minutes.

"What brings you here today?" Bettie said with an empathetic smile, as her crystal clear blue eyes pierced through me, but in a soft, engaging way.

"I'm not really sure," I said. "Your waiting room is the best smelling, calm place I've ever been to. I think I just want to spend the hour in there."

"What about it helps you to feel so calm?" she asked like a therapist who already knows how to guide me away from my obvious deflection.

"The soft music, the book of quotes by Mr. Rogers, and that surf wax candle!! My God it's like a transcendental saturnalia. Maybe I can just set up camp in there and skip this whole therapy thing."

"Is that what you really want?" she said almost baiting. "To just skip this whole therapy thing?"

"Well actually," I replied, "I just want to skip to the middle."

Bettie has helped me in countless ways since that time. So much so that I cannot possibly fit it all into one book. In an effort to stay focused and not dilute my message, I will stick to the ways in which she helped me with the big D.

After being in the depths of grief and confusion for many, many weeks post the D bomb, she said the sentence that would forever be emblazoned on my mind and set a path of growth and personal change. "Loving a person is not a reason to spend your days with them."

Mic drop! "Fucking Hell, Bettie, where did that come from!?"

"I'm not really sure," she said. "It just dropped from the sky and came out of my mouth. I have never said or heard that before."

Was it divine intervention? Was it her expertise as a therapist combined with knowing me for almost a decade? She had certainly heard all the ups and downs of my marriage up until that point, and had even met my husband during one of my sessions. She had insight, therapeutic acumen, and a distinct knowledge of, well, me. She seemed to have stirred all of that in one beautiful boiling pot of intuition and delivered a sentence so meaty that it would take me months to fully unpack.

I looked at her stunned. "So you can love a person, and then just choose to not spend your time with them!?"

"When the situation warrants it, yes," she said. "It happens all the time in all types of different relationships." She went on to explain how some relationships become toxic, and the only way to preserve what is left of them is to create boundaries so clear that the toxicity can no longer hurt you.

"Your love for your ex-husband was undoubtedly there. You never have to deny that or question it. That love is there for you to keep and remember. But spend your days with him? You were hurting, Bern, and you no longer need to do that."

This concept was so transformative for me because before the mic drop bomb of a sentence from Bettie, I thought that the only way to let him go was to make sense of the love part of it. Did I love him too much? Not enough? Did I not show it enough? Did I show it too much? When did it fade? Why did it fade for him and not for me? The trouble in those first few weeks post separation was that I was still in love with him and I had been living under the pretense that love was a reason to stay with someone. Love is what makes the world go round, right? Love is the reason we get up in the morning and do the crazy things that make it all worthwhile. Why wouldn't love be the reason to stay in a marriage? Well, love and two kids.

This mind numbing, jaw dropping, epiphany of a sentence changed that for me. Love is not a reason to spend your days with someone. I was under the delusion that if you love someone, all you need is effort and the combination of the two will produce a functioning relationship. That just seems so simple and pure that it has to be true. Right?

Nope. Not after you hear "the sentence." Bettie continued to explain the sentence so that I would understand it intellectually. Intellect first, emotions later. She told me how dysfunction happens all the time in loving relationships and provided textbook examples where people would have to create boundaries even if it pained them to do so. Examples of how people come to terms with how the relationship is affecting their personal being. I began connecting the dots by seeing how people can love, but also recognize that no love is worth the detriment of the soul.

What Bettie was helping me to see was that my relationship with my ex had become toxic. Love cannot and does not override toxicity. I was living under that fallacy that what the relationship needed was more. More time, more communication, more effort, and more involvement. When an issue would arise, my first thought was always, *Wow, we really need to talk this one through. Let's just apply the rule of more and we can work through everything.* It turns out that more of all of these things did not provide long-term relief. It provided short-term relief and two people exhausted from more frustration and more moments of lost communication. The love was there, but the ability to coexist was diminishing with every conversation that led to nowhere.

The answer to repairing a toxic relationship is not pouring on more of the ingredient that caused the toxicity. The answer has nothing to do with reparations at all. The answer is acknowledging that regardless of where your love for your ex resides, it is time to start spending your days without that person. Spend your days with your kids, friends, family, co-workers, your work, your pets, your routine, and your breaks from your routine. Create the space for you to emerge without him. The time to begin doing that is right now. It is always right now. That love will exist back in the place that it belongs. But today, in this moment, you have the power to spend your days on your own journey.

Gather Your Resources In Summation:

- We all know it takes a village to raise a child, but it also takes a village to get divorced. If you want to do more than survive, you need your village around you.

- Look inward for the strength you already have.

- Pick up the phone and call your friends, family, therapist, lawyer, and any other professional who is there to help.

- Join support groups, sports teams, book clubs, and social groups.

- Know where your strength is and call upon it.

CHAPTER TWO

WAVES OF EMOTION

SURRENDER

With the strength you have gathered by putting your team in place, you are ready for your next spiritual step of surrender. This one takes some unpacking. To surrender to a situation, one must agree that the situation exists, even if it wasn't wanted. This does not take place in a day or in one sitting, but begins and matures over time. Surrender started for me on the morning of the Ghost of Relationship Present when I decided to accept the reality of the situation and stop tugging at something that was no longer mine.

When I woke up after my night at Rachel's house, my mind was set on a new trajectory. I knew that I could never go back to the place of denial again. I had to stop bargaining with fate in an attempt to make life stay static. I couldn't explain all of this to my friends. I needed to point myself in the direction home and start living out the more painful truth of an inevitably dissolving marriage. I hugged my friends goodbye, gathered my tired children, and drove back into my life. I had a feeling of fullness and calm. Mostly because my children were with me and there was nothing more satisfying than knowing you just provided your children with an amazing sleepover experience with their friends. With KIDZ BOP blasting on the radio, I sang to them with all my might. Why not relish in singing Halsey, that has been rerecorded by children, and sung from the backseat by children, all of whom are tone deaf and absolutely nothing like the original Halsey. This method of parenting worked with such ease because it also provided a much needed singing outlet. Singing is one of those activities that I often advise for my patients. Especially the ones who can actually sing. Singing is breathing I tell them. Singing is a great way to be present minded and a way to quiet the chatter that often exists in the human brain. The fact that I am rather tone deaf was of no consequence for this particular circumstance. I took my own advice and sang as passionately as I could. The car drove on through the cold winter day like a mobile cacophony of live streaming pop songs.

With just a short leg of our car trip left, my wonderful tired children fell asleep. Quietude descended upon the car just at the moment I drove back into our beach town. I could smell the sea air and what that scent represented in my life. I wanted to point my SUV in any direction other than home. How could I go home with the realization that was now emblazoned on my brain? How could I go home knowing that the only possible path was to let him go? How on earth does a person let ten years of marriage fall away to dust? I always had such a fighting spirit, and the idea that it was time to stop fighting and start healing took me by a train wreck of a surprise. With one last check in the rearview mirror to make sure the littles were sleeping, I let the torrent that had been building inside of me release like a tidal wave. Holy fuck did those tears come crashing through my brain and on to my very saturated heated steering wheel. The most amazing part was that just when I thought there couldn't possibly be any more tears left in my eyes, another wave came to set a new record. This was the surrender.

Sometimes the next right step was action. Sometimes the next right step was feeling the emotions with all of their intensity as they are, without trying to change them. The next wave of emotion brought a combination of the two. I opened the window (action) and let the salty sea air in. I let it be the reminder that I needed to let him go (feeling emotion). I had surrendered to this situation and this emotional state, and concurrently realized I could not proceed with either of those two things while holding on to him so tightly. Letting him go meant accepting that we were no longer a couple, one entity, with paths that were conjoined. Letting him go meant no longer seeking his advice, approval, and thoughts on life's random circumstances. It meant not calling him, not smelling his soap that was still in our bathroom, and not looking for the moment when he would cup his hands over his mouth when the laughter made it hard to breath. Letting him go meant choosing a life lived from a new perspective, and not letting anything distract me from my intentions. I could not come to these realizations before surrendering to the feelings that brought them. Surrendering to a feeling is not just having a feeling, but bringing your awareness to that feeling and deciding to have it anyway. It is being aware that you are sad and giving yourself the time to feel sad and not judging yourself for feeling that way.

In the car I felt sad. Every breath reminded me of all that I was losing. I did not want to judge myself for the emotion, but man those emotions were intense! It was the sheer intensity that would have brought me to my knees if I hadn't been driving with two sleeping children in the back. All of this "surrendering to the emotion" was proving to be easier said than done. People always say "scream if you need to," but what do you do when you don't want to wake up your littles? What do you do when the situation doesn't lend itself to emotional outbursts? I put the window down again to hit myself with another burst of cold air. Only this time a pocket of snow hit me in the side of the face from a passing car. It felt rude and altogether unneeded, until it didn't. It was yet another situation that I didn't ask for, didn't want, and left me feeling cold and uncomfortable. However, it was a situation that was completely within my ability to handle. I needed to stop, drop, and roll into all the spiritual reading I had done thus far. "Stop, Bernie, your thoughts are not who you are."

It is one thing to learn this lesson, and another to put it into practice during times of high emotion. I thought about the rational understanding of the separateness between being and thinking, and I watched my emotions like a bubble floating by me. This helped me to distance myself from the emotions. I breathed them in, I felt them hard, and I let them go. I truly believe that all of my spiritual gurus are on to something with this. Denying or suppressing the emotions will only make them come back tenfold at another time. But truly feeling them and recognizing them as exactly what they were, a wave of feelings that come and go, I could feel the intensity build and wash away. Letting him go was going to be one of the hardest things I would ever have to do in this life, but knowing that I only had to do it one wave at a time was a lifesaving realization.

"Handle this wave, Bernie, just this one," I let myself tell myself. "This moment is difficult but truly handleable and since you know how to breath, you got this." I reminded myself to stay present and bravely feel all the feels.

I wiped my eyes clear enough to see my way to my driveway. With my sleeping four-year-old in my arms, and my groggy seven-year-old's hand in mine, I brought them up to yet another dinosaur bed and the three of us collapsed into foggy, needed sleep.

I have counseled my patients on this from the standpoint of a skill. Creating distance between who you truly are, and the emotions you are feeling is a wonderful skill to practice. It is even more affirming when you are able to apply the skill during times of high emotion (the time that life skills tend to fall by the wayside). In the past when I taught this skill, I didn't have such a clear personal experience from which to draw insight. I had the reference of significant emotional waves, but not quite the steady supply that hit me so many times post marital separation.

It is not at all a requirement for the therapist to have been through what their patient is going through in order to identify, empathize, and treat the particular ailment. If that were the case, we would all need to be diagnosed with every malady in the book. This is an understandable impossibility and the ramifications of which would leave any person with quite a bit to work through before actually being a therapist. During my field work, which is a time when therapists are not fully licensed but are working "in the field" under heavy supervision, I came across this situation for the first time. My patients were a married couple who needed help with how to parent their rebellious teenager. I did the best I could by sighting (literally) textbook examples of how other parents handled similar situations. They seemed adequately happy with the session, thanked me, and made their next appointment for the following week vowing to report their progress with their daughter. I smiled and waved and kept my inner turmoil sufficiently hidden. My confidence drained with every post-session critique at my performance on a subject with which I had so little personal experience. How could I give advice on parenting when, at the time, I was not yet a parent myself?

I immediately called my mentor and asked for an impromptu supervisory session. All therapists have a supervisor during their field work. This is a person who has a deep understanding of all your cases and can advise as to where your therapeutic progress is heading and how to enhance it. My supervisor gave me advice that day that shook my confidence into the place of professionalism that it needed to be. "You are a professional, Bernadette. You have studied these situations on a graduate level and have demonstrated a mastery understanding of them. Your personal life experience, or lack thereof, has nothing to do with your ability to apply what you have learned from the research, teachings, and experiences of your professional career." I knew what he was getting at. I needed to quiet my mind and my inner critic and focus on what I knew to be the going understanding of adolescent psychology, combined with a lifetime of empathic skills. What I can see now, as a more seasoned therapist and person who has been a parent for many years, is that my therapeutic approach with that couple did not need to change one bit. My personal experience of being a parent might enhance my general understanding of the situation, but it would not in any way change my professional approach to it. My mentor was absolutely correct, and his words of wisdom crossed my path at the perfect time. At one point or another, every therapist feels like a fraud. Am I really allowed to have influence on another person's life and decision making process? What makes me qualified? We all need a person, a mentor, to remind us of that degree that hangs effortlessly on our wall. Just the fact that I wanted it puts me in a category of people who want to dedicate a portion of our lives to the art and sentient characteristics of compassion. It is this deep compassion that relegates personal life experience as irrelevant. I see you, the therapists say, regardless of my past, I see you.

I was thinking about my mentor and his words to me so many years prior. If life experience is irrelevant, then how can I use this tsunami of emotional upset to make me a better therapist and overall better person? Will the ability to coach this skill come to me more readily and viscerally? Will I be able to describe the details of creating space within emotion in a more connected manner? Maybe it isn't the actual experience that I needed but the reminder of the skill that was most useful in my practice. But then the voice came on in my head once again. The voice I wanted to ignore but knew was too loud to ever go unheard. "You are thinking again, Bern. There is simply no need. Get out of this dinosaur bed and sleep in your own room."

SLEEP

Moments after giving birth to my second daughter, I died. I saw no white light, no pearly gates, just blackness. The only shocking aspect for me was how much I didn't try to hold on to life. I saw the busy scramble of nurses and doctors all around me. I heard the loud beeping of monitors and someone yelling "code blue," preceded by more people and more noises. My brand new baby, Mavis, was swiftly taken off my chest and replaced by cold stethoscopes. I didn't even have the strength to reach out my arms and grab her back. Some part of me knew she needed to be some place safer than in my arms. They were already lifeless and unable to rise to the job of motherhood. And then the force came in strong. It was a force that closed my eyes and ended the pain I was feeling in my body. The force knew before I did that every ounce of my energy needed to be put toward survival. The blackness seemed inevitable, and I could do nothing but succumb to it. It enveloped me in stillness and pain-free silence. The hospital lights, the beeping, the room full of so many people, all faded away. Who among us would not succumb to that?

The silence ended with the sound of the midwife's voice. "You are ok, Bernadette. You and your baby are perfectly healthy." Her cadence was so strong, confident, and nurturing. Not one bit of nervousness or fearfulness. Apparently, she had been saying those calm strong words the entire time I was out while she stitched me up. After the birth a problem occurred; a ton of blood was lost, but she fixed the problem with swiftness and skill, and calmed my fears upon reentering the world. I heard her words and felt safe. I saw my husband holding our baby on the other side of the room, and then I passed out again.

The scene repeated itself. The calming voice, the ability to open my eyes, and the heartbeat of the room all came back to me. I still didn't know what was going on or why I died, but I knew that life was coursing through me. Someone handed me my baby and my arms became an extension of motherhood once again. My powerful, living arms brought her tiny body up to my face and there was nothing in this world other than her, me, and the smell of her baby head. The doctors and nurses continued to do their work, and she and I lay quiet, holding, breathing. We did it baby girl. You and I. We triumphed.

Later that night in a different room, she lay in her hospital-issued bassinet next to me in my steel framed bed. The lights were low, the hospital was quiet, and I gathered that it must have been the middle of the night. I knew that I needed sleep as my body ached for it, but my heart was beating so fast that no amount of deep breathing could help me feel calm. I felt like I had just done a speed ball at that point of a party where everyone else goes to sleep. I was confused and thought I might be dying again, so I called the overnight nurse in.

She came in, sneakers squeaking on the floor, fast paced and mission focused.

"My heart," I said. "It's beating so fast, what is happening?"

"It's ok," she said. "You have lost so much blood that your heart has to work twice as hard to deliver oxygen to the rest of your body. That fast pace is just your heart doing its job."

"Ok," I said as I let that information settle. "And what about my baby. She is whimpering and not sleeping. Don't newborns usually sleep the first night?"

"They usually do, yes. But she is perfectly ok. Her vitals are strong and her color is perfect. She is just restless."

I asked the nurse to hand her to me. I didn't know why she was so restless, but I knew that I needed her close in order to figure it out. She delicately picked up my baby, laid her on my chest, and squeaked her way out of the room with a bouncy pivot. This part, this wonderful, intimate, overwhelming part was only between my brand new baby and me.

Her face looked stressed even though I had recently nursed her, and her diaper was clean. My thoughts were not giving me any guidance so I let my instincts take over. My hand started at her head and I could feel the incredible softness of her hair. My lips could feel the skin on her forehead as I gave her a motherly kiss, closed my eyes, and blocked out everything else in the room. My hand then felt the scratchy (in comparison) hospital blanket wrapped around her. My arms, with their limited blood and years of experience, unwrapped her blanket and laid her skin to skin against my chest.

Her whimpering stopped. She nestled right in and immediately fell asleep. This time, with her in my arms, the blackness came again, but in a completely different way. This time it was sweet soft sleep, and my embrace held her close and protected. It wasn't just for her. It was for us both. We needed each other to feel the calm. Her breath was perfect and rhythmic. The first gift she gave me was to choose to be born with me as her mother, and the second was her closeness and presence, thereby inducing the sweetest, softest, much needed sleep.

In the months that followed that pattern held true. Sleep just didn't come for either of us unless she was on my chest. My days were filled with all the joy and difficulties of raising a newborn and a toddler, and my nights were spent with her nestled into the place that brought us both the elixir that we needed.

As her newborn body gained weight, she learned to sleep on her own. As my body repaired itself from childbirth I learned to sleep on my own as well. Many years later she still is one of the best sleepers I have ever known. She passes right out like clockwork, and wakes up exactly ten hours later.

I had a similar 7-8 hour sleeping regime until the stress of marital separation. Once the gravity of the upheaval hit between the eyes, I found myself feeling exactly like I did in that hospital room. No amount of deep breathing could calm my anxious heart. No amount of meditation or even Ambien could knock me out. I felt I needed to succumb again, but this time not to the emerging blackness, but to the fact that my eyes were wired open. My brain could not let this one go.

As my baby turned four, she could not process what my half empty bed actually meant. She only saw it as an opportunity to have a sleepover with Mama. I lost the will to keep my resolve of "you have your bed and I have mine" attitude. As an experienced mother, I knew that the decision to let her sleep with me would lead to an onslaught of repeated "you let me do it last time" requests. This is a difficult call and one every parent must make at some point. Unable to sift through the pros and cons of such a decision, I let her hop right into bed with me for a sleepover. I was tired and feeling mom guilt and just wanted to make her happy.

As I lay there questioning if this decision was going to come back to bite me, I heard her drift into whispering sleep. Her rhythmic presence once again filled the room and brought with it the graceful touch of peace.

Her body was 40 pounds heavier than the last time she showed me it was all going to be ok, but her baby's breath was exactly the same. There was a part of me (and every parent) who would always see her baby innocence within her no matter what age she grew into. I knew as long as I could hear her breathing, as long as I could feel the life in my tired arms, we were going to get through it all together. I did not sleep. This time I just listened, over and over, to her chest as it rose and fell. Her breath was my reminder that my ability to stay alive, to supply oxygen to my arms, to not fade to blackness, and to carry out the gift that was given to me at her birth, was all that I needed. We did it, baby girl. You, your sister, and I. We triumphed.

Sleep was difficult while managing the stress of divorce. There was no way around that. The struggle for sleep seemed endless. In time, I developed an overall elixir that helped get me through some very stressful times. Mavis's breath helped me to feel close and connected to that which I valued most. It also helped to quiet the chatter in my mind that liked to get louder at night.

For everyone experiencing dark times, it is important to know that it will all work out in the long run. Sleep will come as it needs to, and worrying about it will not help. Comfort yourself and surrender to knowing that there are times when sleep will not come as easily. Make your typical "sleep hours" as comfortable as possible with anything that you find relaxing. Do what you can to sleep, follow a smart sleep hygiene regime, and then let it go.

Sleep hygiene tips:

1. No TV screens at least an hour before bed. They block your production of melatonin (your natural sleep hormone). Listen to a podcast or read a book.
2. Take a 20-minute bath or shower one hour before bed. The change in temperature will promote melatonin and help to set your circadian rhythm.
3. Meditate. Guided or unguided.
4. Go to a doctor or therapist to discuss prescription and non-prescription sleep medications. Sometimes you will find an elixir that works. Sometimes you won't. It's all ok.
5. Some products that help people include: sleep lamps, lavender aromatherapy, CBD oil, and many others. Do a search online and see what jumps out at you.
6. Remember to take the pressure off. This is a stage that will not last forever.

SPACES

Part of adulting is doing things that we truly don't want to do, but we know we must. I don't like to pull the hair that formulates on the shower drain, but I know that I must. The sight of any type of mold on food makes me want to run for the hills, but instead I gather up the nastiness, and do what needs to be done. When completing any of these actions that require perseverance, the thoughts in my mind include, *act now, think later*. Meaning, don't process the ickiness now, this action needs to be done and your thoughts, no matter how valid, will only slow the process. Take a breath, be an adult, and get that shit done.

Some of these actions are more apparent than others. For example, you will not be able to drive the car until you scrape the snow from the windshield. Hurdles like this are obvious and life will not continue on the path that you want it to until they are done. The other type, the less obvious tacit hurdles, are the ones that are so much more difficult because life can go on perfectly well without completing them. Quite often, no one but you will know whether you get them done or not. Well, in my case, no one but me and a very detail-oriented friend named Ellie, also known as Ghost of Relationships Past.

Maybe it was not so much that she was detail oriented, but more that she knew to speak up about the things that she noticed, no matter how difficult, because it was part of being a good friend. Sometimes the hard conversations were not pleasurable, but they needed to be had. I've seen her do it so many times throughout my life that I know her process. First, she looks off into the distance as if gathering her thoughts.

Then she reaches her dainty arm, clinking with designer bangles, for whatever liquid was apropos for the time. In high school it was a juice box, in college it was a Long Island Iced Tea, and in adulthood any combination of coffee, wine, or smoothie. With her satisfying drink in hand, she delivered the hard truth with love and didn't mince words. Thank goodness she became an attorney.

On this particular Sunday morning, we were just coming out of a Barre class. I had slept over the night before with my kids, and her husband graciously offered to watch all of the children so that she and I could exercise and have time to chat over smoothies and coffee. With sweat still dripping from our brows, she set the stage. At a long and tumultuous six weeks past separation, I was still so tired from yet another sleepless night, but was enjoying the warmth of the coffee on a rather cold winter morning. The velvet chairs were enticing in the hip and trendy breakfast establishment, and Ellie didn't waste time.

"Bernie, you're still wearing your rings."

"Yep, I know," I said as I stared down at them longingly.

"Is that what you need right now?"

"Well, yes," I said defensively. "The kids don't know we are separated yet. I don't want them to figure it out on their own, and if I take my rings off, they will think something's up."

"Don't you get them cleaned? Or even just take them off to go bowling or something? There are a million reasons why people take their rings off. You can choose any one of them so that you don't have to go around with a constant reminder on your hand. Plus, your kids are young. They are not going to put this together."

"I don't know. It's just not a risk I'm willing to take."

My ex and I had been waiting to tell the kids and I didn't know exactly why. It all seems blurred now, but sometimes the heart just needs to postpone the inevitable. Telling the kids took a ton of strength and I needed some time to build it. But walking around with those rings on felt like having a cement arm. They became heavy and extraneous. I didn't realize the brick I was carrying around until Ellie mentioned it. She held up a mirror and delicately asked me to look at it and decide if there was anything off with the picture.

The issue for me was that there were so many things off with the picture. I was way too thin and there were bags under my eyes. I had just completed an exercise class that I had zero energy for and fudged my way through. I was so afraid to live my life so I kept escaping it and driving the three hours to her house so that I could be in someone else's town/life/home. She welcomed it with open arms but it wasn't a long term answer.

"Here's the thing," I said to her after contemplating the mirror she just put in my face, "I don't know what I'm doing here. Really, I don't know why I keep coming to Long Island, I don't know why I take exercise classes that I can't possibly participate in, and I don't know why I order food that my wrangled stomach can't possibly finish; I just do. I am faking it until I make it. I feel like a shell of myself, but Faith told me that my light is still strong and I believe her. I have to believe her because it's all I have to go on. This is the hardest battle of my life and I have to win it. I have to come out stronger. If not for me, for them."

"I get it. I know you'll take your rings off when you're ready. I just know that you're hurting and I want to help you through it," she said.

"Thanks El, but fuck I wish you lived closer. The Belt Parkway is killing me."

Later that night back in good ol' Jersey while the kids were asleep, I sat in my bedroom listening to the deafening silence emanating from it. Everything had changed, but somehow I was among the same bedding, same furniture, and same pictures on the walls. All was the same except one giant living breathing entity that had always seemed essential to the make-up of family life.

I looked down at my rings. "Fine!" I thought. "Act now, process later. This shit needs to be done." The act of taking rings off was miniscule and took seconds, but my heart didn't process it that way.

Once those rings were off, everything else seemed off as well. I looked around the light airy coastal style bedroom that I had always loved. Suddenly, all the decor seemed anachronistic and misplaced. I had no idea there was still a wedding picture hanging on my wall. How did I not see that before? The book case was filled with memories and trinkets six weeks past their due date and I could finally see the heaviness they brought to the room.

I called Ellie because I didn't know what else to do. "I did it. They're off. But I don't feel empowered. I feel sad and now my hand feels less than. Less pretty, less adorned, and less loved. And to make matters worse, everything is wrong now. I want to escape these walls that are filled with so many memories of him but I can't. I want to strip it all bare. Seems crazy, but I want my room to feel as naked as my finger."

"So do it," she said. "Get rid of all of it. That's not crazy at all! Every item that reminds you of him or your life together, put it in a box and forget about it. You can't change the actual room right now but you can change everything in it."

I got to work with her still on the phone. I didn't want to live another moment in a room saturated in his scent. This took a surprisingly short amount of time. A few boxes were transported out of the room and I was feeling satisfied. Not altogether happy, but content with a job well done.

"This feels strangely good, Ellie. All that stuff in those boxes was weighing me down. But now, the next problem. I am staring at a closet that has his stuff in it. I don't know what's worse, a closet filled with all his stuff, or a closet with blank spaces in it where his stuff used to be?"

"Oh, I will help you fill those spaces!" She said without missing a beat. "They will be the trendiest, coolest clothes, and you will look great in them and they will be all about your new chapter." She was not kidding! Her knack for fashion is like nothing I have ever seen. Not only that, but her eidetic memory pairs new clothes with existing ones from my wardrobe that I don't even remember.

"Ok, I'm on it," I said. The new life will look great on me.

Filling those spaces took time, but they needed to be spaces first. You can't put new items in place until the old ones are removed. I bought myself some new bedding and found an extremely feminine pink butterfly to put in the place where the wedding photo used to hang. Ellie truly did help me to fill those spaces in my closet. Not necessarily with clothes, but by being there with me as she and our other two girlfriends dressed up and posed for a picture. The four of us were laughing and leaning on each other. That picture is now framed and emanates style and friendship, and sits proudly on my closet shelf.

I bought canvases and painted a sunset on a portion of them. I then handed the paintbrush to my four-year-old and asked her to help me with the rest. She looked at me with disbelief that I was going to let her paint on my painting, but she grabbed the brush, dipped it into a huge glob of indigo, and let her inner Picasso run wild. Pure joy seeped through her pores as color after color hit the canvas. She giggled with each stroke and created an ocean of paint. I snapped a photo of her while she was doing it, and now that photo is on my nightstand, and the four large paintings centered above my bed is a constant reminder of what is truly important. Those paintings represent so much love and creativity among my three-person family, and they changed the energy of the room to reflect the new chapter I was heading into.

This is an integral part of surrender. By wiping the slate clean, you are admonishing that you have a slate, and that it deserves to be cleaned. You have a home that is all you, be it a room, an apartment, your mom's place, or an entire house. You have an area that you have carved out to be your own and it is time to make it that way. You deserve those new sheets no matter how extraneous the purchase may feel. There are also plenty of ways to buy new/used items to fit your budget because, over all, your mental health is worth it. It's worth the search, it's worth the money, and it's worth the effort.

There is no exact timeline for getting this done, so I will just say do it sooner rather than later. If you are the one who left the home, or if both you and your ex left at the same time, then there is less for you to do, but you can still start right away to make your new space your own. Get some pictures in frames, travel somewhere and buy something that represents your new adventure, and then take it home to your new space.

Books, clothes, decor, pictures. These are all items that can be bought, salvaged at a flea market, borrowed, or made. Budget is not an excuse. Take a deep breath, be an adult, and get that shit done. Onward.

Waves of Emotion In Summation

- The first step in managing your emotions is to surrender to them. Truly feel them and manage them one wave at a time.

- Get some sleep and/or meditate, whichever one comes first. Sometimes emotions need the shut off valve too.

- Acknowledge your emotional state in a physical sense by creating space to heal, preferably in your bedroom.

CHAPTER THREE

RELATIONSHIP AUTOPSY

TRA

To truly benefit from the end of any relationship, it is necessary to do what I call The Relationship Autopsy. You will need to put the metaphorical relationship on the coroner's table and sharpen your scalpel. This is going to hurt, but what you will discover is worth the time it takes to put each of the relationship's vital organs under the microscope to come up with a true cause of death, and subsequent rebirth. Any long relationship has chapters, times of high connectivity and times of carving your own path. This is a natural part of the ebb and flow of a continuing partnership with another person. But there are times when those two can be a bit too extreme. Those are the moments, the vital organs, that we will be dissecting.

This is not to place blame, but more to figure out why those arguments got a little too loud, or those doors were slammed a little too hard. Or it could be that the dinners became a bit too quiet, and one or both of you rolled away instead of toward. When did the natural ebb and flow turn into the waves that brought the tsunami? How did you contribute to the end, and how are you going to own your part in it? If you were the breaker, were there aspects of the person that didn't match with you that you could have seen or addressed sooner? If you are the breaky, did you see it coming? And if not, what could have been some of the signs that you missed?

Before we completely slide into the perilous "whys," it is important to remember that there are parts of this that are no fault. Sometimes the end has nothing to do with either person, just on the relationship itself. When two people are no longer compatible, they will not bring out the best in the other. And in some cases, two incompatible people who are spending an inordinate amount of time with each other will bring out the absolute worst in the other. There are times when, for no fault of either person, the relationship has just run its course. In these times, it is both prudent and wise to recognize the chasm that simply cannot be bridged, and do what is necessary before it all becomes ugly.

The day after a big sports game, any player who has access to footage of the game will make use of its benefits. They will pick apart the game day replay in slow motion during the high and low points of the game. They do this to learn from mistakes and celebrate the wins. There are always ways the player could have stepped left or right to improve his game. In relationships, there are always ways you could have communicated better, listened more, and stepped up your role as a partner. Some of the questions you can ask yourself include the following:

1. Did I really hear my ex?
2. Did I consider my ex's needs as equal to my own?
3. Was the end really the end?
4. When did the end actually start?
5. Was I aware of the moments that seemed off?
6. If not, am I aware of them now?
7. Would I have handled them differently?
8. Did I act in any way that seemed misaligned with my character?
9. What, if anything, would I have done differently, and why?
10. Are there any open wounds that need to be addressed?
11. Were there moments when I held on too tightly but should have let go?
12. Were there moments when I let go that I should have stood my ground?

13. What is the baggage, the parts of me, that I don't want to bring into my next relationship?

This part is not easy. It requires you to dissect the parts of the relationship that many would prefer to forget. But this corpse of a relationship contains many hidden gems and it would be a shame to waste them. These gems will not reveal an iron clad way to never lose a relationship again. Quite the opposite in fact. This exercise will show you more about yourself. The more you know about yourself and what makes you tick, the more complete you can be in all your roles. You are a being in the process of self-actualizing, and this will put you further on that road.

THE HEART

One of the gems discovered during my relationship autopsy was the battle between mind and body. When your thoughts and your body are at odds, go with your body. It knows best.

To fully examine and absorb, I will put the heart on the coroner's table.

There are a few luxuries in this world that I find truly uplifting. When splurging on a luxury, I have always preferred experiences over things. A special night away over a piece of jewelry. Quality time over material items.

So, when Ex and I were given tickets to a hot Broadway show as a Christmas gift, I could not have been more overjoyed. We booked a swanky hotel, reservations for dinner, and decided to make a Manhattan night out of it. Our kids were happy to be spending the night with Ali, the super fun babysitter, and we were happy to get away for the night. Time was the highest luxury of them all, and we were right in the middle of a very busy work season for both of us, and desperately needed time as a couple.

The scene was set perfectly. We put our luggage in our room and headed down to the hotel bar that personified the confluence of sophistication and coolness. The eco-friendly hand towels matched the cucumber-infused water. The living herb wall delicately garnished every drink with freshness and air purified vitality. The energy of Manhattan matched the energy of two married people who were excited to have the opportunity to spend time together and enjoy the night.

It was still early in the evening and the crowd was starting to take shape. He took me by the hand and we weaved in and out of the people waiting for their tables. He grabbed the last two seats at the end of the bar just in time. We ordered our Kettle and club, and chatted about how different this hotel was from its sister hotel in Miami. Different city, same hotel. Different night, same couple. Different words, same conversation.

"Did you get those TPS reports done?"

"About those TPS reports."

A few years prior to this Manhattan moment, I began working with Ex at his family business. It turned out that my knack for writing proved beneficial to showcase his work, and the added benefit was that he and I could spend more time together. Basically, we wanted it all. We wanted more time as a couple but also to continue to build the business that he loved so much. We thought we had the winning combination with my marketing skills and his business acumen. We were on fire as a couple as our lives and worlds became increasingly joined with aligned business goals. I didn't mind putting my practice on hold for such a worthy endeavor. Plus, I loved the work and the opportunity to be a part of a growing company.

For years it felt like the component that kept us more connected than ever. I truly did not want it to end, but the difficulties of working together as a married couple crept in during the most inopportune times. It is very difficult for a married couple to work together for many reasons, but highest on the list is that it is just so difficult to shut work mode off when it's time to just enjoy. When time is limited and deadlines are fast and both people are passionate about their role in the big picture, lines get blurred.

What was supposed to be a quick conversation about loose ends at work turned into a heated debate over checklist priorities. Anyone who has been married knows how quickly buttons can be pushed and raw nerves can be triggered. It took us about three sips from our biodegradable straws to go right into the dual of two people who haven't had enough time to hash out life's squabbles, let alone the added squabbles of workplace drama. One misstep compacted the other and we couldn't see ourselves through to the end of it.

I needed a time out. I could feel myself becoming flooded with emotion and I knew a new environment would give me a chance to let my blood pressure come down and reconcile with the present. Like a beacon through the fog, that little skirt wearing stick figure on the door guided me to my personal shrine. The ladies' bathroom contained just enough space from the situation, without being a complete bail out. I was sure that he could see the tears that had formed in my eyes, and I didn't need to hide them as much as send a signal that although emotions were coming, I was taking a moment on my own to handle them. Nothing out of control here, just a moment to reapply lipstick and take a few deep breaths.

As I stared into the wrought iron mirror, the person staring back at me looked so confident and strong, and like she was holding up a dam that was about to break at any moment. My make-up was running down my face by the second because my few tears turned into a flood of disappointment. Were my expectations too high? A night out in the city shouldn't be an assumed good time and break from stress? I stared back at myself in knowing disbelief because too high expectations were not the reason for my disappointment. I was coming to the realization that our situation was simply not working. We were arguing about work so much that it had bled into even the most shiny of evenings. The work arguments started at 6 a.m. upon opening my eyes, and they were continuing in a way that felt out of control. It felt like there was not one moment spared from work details. My attempts to create boundaries around when work should end were clearly not working.

The glow of the ornate chandelier could not hide the defeat in my eyes. Going back to that bar meant subjecting myself to more critiques of my work. Critiques easily handled in the office, but I was realizing that neither of us had the ability to leave those roles at work so that the husband and wife dynamic could emerge. I would remain a subordinate in perpetuity, or leave the position I had worked so hard to attain. As many times as I had tried to find a middle ground, leave the office at the office and be solely husband and wife elsewhere, I could also see the writing on the bathroom mirror. It was written all over my face. This dynamic settled. It was not going away while I remained his employee. I was the marketing director and had a vision of my own, but he would always be the CEO. He was the boss at work with good reason and that was the way it had to be. But I vehemently needed that dynamic to shift back to co-conspirators in all other scenarios. The problem was, that was a difficult role from which to step down. Bossy was bossy and frustrated was frustrated.

Although I was accepting of my frustrations and of the difficulty of the situation, I thought there had to be a way through it. Yes, it's true that most couples claim that they could never work with their spouse, but we were different, weren't we? We were a power couple who could work our way through any obstacle. After all, what could possibly be harder than raising two children together? These thoughts were pervasive as I pushed myself away from the mirror. "You've got this, Bern," I said to myself. "Don't walk away from a great working scenario just because of some turbulence."

With my brain running on high octane, I went looking for my husband. I came back to the bar and saw a kettle/club, and a cherry waiting for me to change the scene. "Let's start over," I said, and I meant it. Reboot the night and be thankful that we have a sitter. He could not have been more happy to do exactly that. "Why did we even bring work up?" one of us said while the other grabbed a drink to cheers the notion.

Sometimes there's just no better word than "cheers!" That word has a tendency to bring people right into the moment. The word signifies a call to take a look at the people around you, acknowledge the joy in your company, and share the experience of taking the first sip of that particular drink. In many Latin cultures it is customary to make sure that you make eye contact with every person you are "cheersing," because according to superstition, whoever does not make eye contact will not get laid that evening. Aside from the fun aspect of this custom, it seems to take the tacit attempt to acknowledge your company, and make it overt. As if to say "pay attention, asshole, this is a good moment, and it's your life, so pay some respect and be in it!"

We let our salute to the moment bring us right back to where we were. Which happened to solidly not be the office in our tiny suburban town. We were in Manhattan, on date night, not talking about work. He was not running a job site and I was not finding creative ways to showcase his work. We were not having a conversation about ROMI (return on marketing investment), and we were not discussing if our new billboard was making more of an impact than the last one. But most importantly, we were not arguing about how many emails were sent to Anderson Windows about our co-branding attempts and whether or not we were putting sufficient energy into said endeavor. Instead of letting these points journey out of our minds, we let them become the giant elephant in the room. Looming, waiting, our two ton elephant was sitting on a tiny chair, and with just the slightest movement, would bring the whole damn restaurant down.

"New bar," I said. "We must just need a new bar." We ventured out into the night with new fervor and a slight buzz. This was Manhattan. Anything could happen. Any conversation could lead to new heights. We were walking at a strong pace with the crisp, cool April air keeping us fresh. I don't usually like walking in heels (or standing in them for that matter), but on this Manhattan night, I didn't seem to mind. The glitz and glam of Broadway had a contagious nature that made the night seem energized. I wanted to laugh and smile and hold my charming husband's hand.

We arrived a few minutes early for our reservations at a hip new sushi bar. Since our show started at eight, our reservations were a bit early for the usual Saturday night Manhattan crowd. There was no one sitting at the bar and the sushi bar tender was still setting up the tools necessary for the people who were not yet there. It gave a feeling like being the first ones rolling into a party and the host was still setting up.

"That's ok," I said. "A bit more quiet and intimate never hurt anyone." I was excited and hungry and didn't mind the lack of crowd at all; but one look at him told a different story.

This time it wasn't about the conversation, but the lack of it. We tried to muddle through. Some words were exchanged. There were no reboots left. Instead, we hit an emotional nerve that was way too raw and sent shock waves to an already depleted emotional bank account. The serve and volley of marital discourse took moments to devolve into the argument we tried so hard to walk away from. The ever changing environment did not save us from the place in which we found ourselves. If we had both been better, maybe it could have been prevented; but we weren't, and it wasn't.

We left the restaurant together, but then did he walk off or did I? Did he throw his hands up in despair and confusion or did I? It doesn't matter. The point is we lost each other. Literally and figuratively as one of us walked off. What was once a kinetic energy in the air of Manhattan turned static and overwhelming. What was once a crisp and cool April night turned into winds that were cold and unforgiving. The noises of the city, once ambient and subtle, turned loud and immutable.

Alone on a city street, I found myself strangely aware of my senses, and haunted by the image I saw of myself in the mirror just moments earlier. I was rendered a woman cool and confident but unable to deny her stream of tears. This was a woman awakening to the fact that something had to give. I was coming to the realization that I couldn't work with my husband and keep our marriage strong at the same time. This was harder to grasp than it seems. So many people had looked at the two of us and uttered some version of "I love my husband, but I could never work with him." I don't know why it took us two and a half years plus countless time, energy, and conversations to figure that out. Part of the mystique of it all was how magical it had been in the beginning. We were an undeniable force the first two years we worked together, but like any storm, that energy needed to come to its ephemeral end.

This was years prior to our divorce, and at that time I did not have the skill of non-resistance that I do now. I was deeply resisting the notion of ending my time working with my husband. That woman from the mirror was screaming, "Wake up, you can save your marriage, but you cannot keep hoping that more of the same will lead to different outcomes!" Basically, nothing changes if nothing changes. I vehemently did not want to hear that, especially from a ghostly mirrored image of myself from moments prior. I wanted to say, "Shut the fuck up you teary-eyed parallel-universe version of myself. Your epiphanies are not wanted here. Why can't I work with him and save my marriage at the same time?" But that was what I like to call resistance, and that resistance to reality, combined with traffic and street lights, led me to my first and only panic attack.

Working with people experiencing panic attacks has actually been one of my favorite maladies to treat because they are so, well, treatable. People have come to my office explaining their panic attacks in a variety of intensity levels. Some people were slightly perturbed by them, and others found them to be so debilitating that their entire lives changed as a result. Some people could no longer go to work, drive on the street, go over bridges, go near hospitals or malls, be alone, be with people, or be by themselves. Some people had been experiencing these panic attacks for years, others only a few times. Many of the panic attack referrals had come from doctors who had informed their patients that they did not have a heart attack, but that they had a panic attack, and a mental health professional was what they needed, not a rush to the emergency room.

The experience of these patients going from the emergency room to my office must have been a mind trip in itself. One minute you are legitimately thinking you are having a heart attack, and the next are in a mental health office being told to breathe through it. It is both humbling and empowering to realize that you have the ability to control the sensation, albeit still scary to feel your body act in a way that is foreign and debilitating.

"The only thing that has ever come from a panic attack is the end of the panic attack." This is one of the first things I tell my patients when they step through my door. It breaks the entire experience down rather succinctly. "But what if I'm driving?! I could kill someone!" "Even when you are driving, I will teach you to focus on your breath and on the road so that even driving will not be a concern," I explain reassuringly.

This is the magical point when my patients and I would begin our beautiful dance. The patient comes up with copious scenarios in which doom will certainly occur, and I continue to debunk these concerns with a blend of confidence and compassion. What I like to call a beautiful dance is most often called 'reframing' by mental health professionals. It is when therapists take a thought that seems catastrophic, and break it down to something more palatable. So, "my heart is beating so fast I must be having a heart attack" turns into "my heart is beating fast because I am feeling some anxiety, with some deep breaths it will return to a slower heart rate." This continues for as long as it takes for the new narrative that has been built upon bodily sensations to form in the person's mind. He or she does not have to believe it right away, but the seed has been planted. Many patients experience a tremendous amount of relief just from this one initial session. The breathing techniques take a while to master, but the effects from just one deep breath can be felt instantly.

I had one patient write his reframed thoughts on a piece of paper in his wallet. When he felt the panic attack begin, he would take out his paper and say the words in his mind, *I am not going to die. I am experiencing mild discomfort but I can handle it. I will slow my breath and let this pass*. He also started wearing a mala bead bracelet. Counting out the beads and feeling their smooth surfaces gave him a sense of relief. He continued to come to the office to do the breath work and within a few weeks his panic attacks decreased dramatically. When they did come, their intensity and duration decreased as well.

These steps are just the beginning of helping people to feel like themselves again. There is certainly more work that needs to be done to help people come home to themselves, but addressing the panic attacks is much like dressing a wound. You must stop the bleeding first. And if a person is experiencing panic attacks on a daily basis, then they are being wiped of energy and personal vitality, and therefore take first priority in treatment. In Maslow's hierarchy of needs, physiology and safety are very base level needs, and the misleading thoughts that often coexist with panic attacks threaten both of them.

That is, except when you are yourself a therapist who specializes in treating panic attacks. Until that point, I had used my well-honed skill of compassion to identify with my patients. As previously discussed, this in itself is sufficient as a therapist. But sometimes we are given a gift of experience that gives us an inside look at the minds we have cared for so deeply in our work. Like a biologist studying an amoeba from the inside out, I was granted the wonderful experience of living my own lovely panic attack.

Cue the sirens, the busy-ness of Times Square, the people rushing by, and my heart beating so fast and so hard it actually hurt my chest. I balanced myself on a street sign and let the wave come. The pain in my chest increased as my lungs struggled to keep up with the demands of my heart. The rest of my body felt winded, weak, and off balance. My hands were sweating despite the cool air. I could see very clearly how all of these physical symptoms could lead someone down a scary and dark path. Especially when these symptoms are brought on by high stress or high emotion situations. The interplay between mind and body is astounding on any day, but especially when experiencing a panic attack. There is this critical moment when your thoughts can positively or negatively impact the physical symptoms. Pain in the chest turns into "I must be having a heart attack," which turns into an even more increased heart rate, which turns into even more pain in the chest. This circuitous thought pattern elongates the duration and intensity of the panic attack, which is often what leaves people feeling thoroughly depleted at its completion. Whereas, what I was thinking at the time, "holy shit balls this is so cool," will break that pattern and significantly decrease the sensation.

I have been meditating and deep breathing for many years, so when I put my hand to my belly and told myself to breathe deeply and slowly, my muscles and lungs instinctively knew just what to do. There is a direct link between heart rate and breath rate, so as the breath slows, so does the heart. I kept my gaze steadily on the parked black BMW in front of me as my body hopped into yogic, trans-like, Buddha in Times Square. As busy New Yorkers rushed by me, my mind was almost giddy with the opportunity that had befallen me. I was not scared at all. I was fascinated by the power of the human body, and intensely curious how long it would take for my heart to match my breath. I continued to think soothing thoughts as if they were a message to my body, "I am here for you, continue to take as long as you need to feel better, everything is ok." My mind and my body became Team Calm. I used the mind/body connection to my advantage and rode that wave until all systems had returned to normal.

The duration was probably no more than five minutes, but the impact was far greater. I not only had the chance to experience a panic attack from the inside out, I had a message from my body, and I received it loud and clear. My body knew before my brain as one's body often does. I could no longer fool myself into thinking that working with my husband was a good thing. I truly did not want the 'power couple' chapter to come to an end, but what the panic attack taught me was that it already had.

I took my hand off the sign post, texted my husband to meet me at the theatre, and walked into the next sea of uncertainty.

With the Panic Attack organ placed gently on the table, I can play that scene over in retrospect. Was it the beginning of the end? No. But it was the beginning of something and the end of something. Working with my ex was a microcosm of our entire relationship. The goods were so good and the bads were so bad. Closing that chapter meant losing the part of our relationship that had become the heartbeat of it. What I couldn't see at the time was that this was the very reason I had to end working with him. I didn't want work to be the heartbeat. I wanted our home, family, and Sunday dinners to be the heartbeat. There was a part of him that wanted the same but the heart is a very difficult organ to replace.

If I skipped over the Relationship Autopsy, I would still have this memory, but I wouldn't have its meaning. I would still keep very sharp details of the coolest panic attack in history in mind as I treat my patients, but I would miss how that panic attack served me on my journey. It taught me to pay attention to the whispers and then shouts of my body. It showed me that my trajectory was all wrong. As a result, I can walk through life more attuned, more dialed in to the messages that are quietly sent as a nudge, and then a roar from somewhere deep inside. The hope is that next time I catch them when they are still in the nudge stage. But if not, that is ok too. I will welcome another panic attack and say, "Hello again, my dear friend, what are you here to teach me this time?"

THE BRAIN

Next organ on the table... the brain.

The beginning is never the beginning, which is why I didn't start there. But if this divorce had a beginning it was with the question, "What has been up with you lately?" The answer I was expecting was something along the lines of "work has been unusually stressful." That was not the answer I got. Instead, the answer at the time seemed rather hopeful and engaging. "I'm not happy, Bern."

I took a moment to think about it. I knew that hearing that he had been stressed at work would have left me with very little opportunity for follow up. There was very little I could do about being stressed at work other than to continue to be a supportive wife. But generally unhappy? Now that was something that this therapist of a wife could really sink her teeth into.

"In what way are you unhappy? Life, work, balancing the two? Give me some deets and I can set about helping you fix it."

"I'm unhappy with us," he replied.

"You're telling me this the night before we are supposed to leave for Costa Rica?"

I thought this particular piece of the puzzle perturbing but not a loss. I had been looking forward to this vacation for so long. It was a celebration of my 40th birthday. It was also a chance to spend some serious time with my husband and explore a new country. What could be more exciting than that? I did not want anything to spoil it or put a dark cloud over it.

I accepted this new twist as part of our journey in marriage together, and was able to put an immediate positive spin on it.

"Actually, this is perfect! We have experienced marital turbulence before and this is no different. The fact that we are going away gives us a chance to really talk things through. We can have some fun while simultaneously devising a plan to help you feel happier and more engaged. We board in eight hours, so let's get some sleep."

"Are you sure, Bern? I realize my timing couldn't be worse."

Not really understanding the question, I replied, "I'm sure. Let's do this."

So now how can I skip through this part of the story? This is the juice. The fun. The gritty, sexy, fiery, meat of it all. We connected in many ways and we were able to talk through the darkness that can sometimes plague a marriage. We devised a plan to set aside time to really talk through the reasons for his unhappiness, and when it felt like too much, go back to the vacationing couple in love that we were. That way we could make progress while still doing all the things that helped us feel connected.

But the details of this part of the story will be skipped. It fell way too heavily on the side of the story of our marriage, and not the side of the story that was our divorce. For him it was more of a goodbye, but I was unaware that we were saying goodbye as we were saying it. Clearly there were details that I missed which made it a very high emotional cliff to fall from. The amount of connectedness that we shared left me feeling that we had weathered the storm. We walked through the airport back to America hand-in-hand, ready to take on the rest of our marriage in a new way. But, he left our home immediately upon our return and I could not have been more blindsided.

That was my reality, but I will remain soaked in neutrality with any perspective therein. Was I blindsided because I didn't want to see the crash that was ahead of me? Did I lose my ability to truly hear what he was saying? Did I fall prey to confirmation bias and only hear the points that I wanted to hear? Probably. Was I blindsided because he kept parts of himself so well hidden that even Magnum P.I. wouldn't see it? Maybe. The overarching point is that it doesn't matter why. Sometimes each person's perception of a situation holds little importance to the experience of it. His intentions were vastly different than my experience. The only point that matters to this story is that the fall hit me so hard I was stripped of all that I knew.

The juxtaposition of being on an incredibly romantic vacation with my husband of ten years, and then having him leave suddenly was a blast that would be hard for anyone to handle. However, I see now that it set me on a trajectory of transformation beyond imaginable.

I have read about these moments many times. Some call it "rock bottom," some call it getting broken down. I tend to call it being stripped bare. Since my world was completely flipped in one moment, I no longer had a sense of time and space. It was like I was blind, and deaf, and living in a world without gravity. I couldn't eat or sleep, but more importantly I couldn't think. None of my thoughts seemed to make any sense, so I just stopped thinking them. My mind went completely blank leaving me with only instinct.

It is amazing how attuned and focused one's instincts can be. As a mother, I could care for my children with laser focus because when I was with them it was like literally nothing else existed in this world. When you only have the capacity to handle that which is directly in front of you, the fluff of unimportant things fall away. "You need some help on your math homework darling? No problem, absolutely nothing else exists for me other than this second grade math equation. I'm all over it. Actually, the second I step away from your homework, my world becomes a fiery mess, so is there anything else I can help you with?" Those were not the words that came from my mouth but that was the sentiment behind them which caused me to be unshakably attentive. The adrenaline coursing through my body gave me the ability to be up for days and miraculously not feel tired. Did I turn into the bionic woman? Why do any of us get sleep anyway if we can feel so not tired without it?

Adrenaline is a powerful hormone in both its physical attributes and the psychological message it sends. According to Wikipedia, the key actions of adrenaline "include increasing the heart rate, increasing blood pressure, expanding the air passages of the lungs, enlarging the pupil in the eye, redistributing blood to the muscles, and altering the body's metabolism, so as to maximize blood glucose levels (primarily for the brain)."

Physically, this gave me the ability to just get through it. Parenting doesn't stop just because you are going through something. Food doesn't shop itself. Boo boos need bandages, and basically life moves on. Caffeine doesn't quite cut it, so adrenaline helps. But the psychological message is equally as important. Act now, process later. You will have time to emotionally handle this in pieces, so for now get your shit done and let the emotional part happen with whatever timing you need.

I was able to manage my day with extremely little sleep, but by no means was I bringing my best self. At one point I stood outside of the shower, naked, with my hand outstretched checking the temperature of the water. My body felt slightly cold and slightly wet and I could not remember for the life of me if I was heading into the shower or just getting out of it. At that moment I had no direction and no memory. The only information my brain was taking in was the current temperature of the water on my hand. I decided that it seemed warmer under the water than standing outside of it, so I went in. This was a very base level form of decision making and I was completely unaware that this state was also very spiritual.

We have seen it play out in history so many times. St. Francis of Assisi stripped himself of all of his worldly possessions and went on to be one of the most venerated religious figures in history. Siddartha (Buddha) walked away from all of his family's comforts with nothing so that he could experience the world from and with nothing. Nothingness is often revered as one of the most transformative states because it puts you in a place of complete control of all that comes within your circle. You block out all that is negative and only let in what works for you.

Walking around as the shell of myself gave me the ability to firmly block out all noise. I knew that I only had the emotional bandwidth to care for myself and my children, and all extraneous stressors would need to be cut from my purview. When news would come on the television, I turned it off because news is a stressor for which I had zero control, and was deemed outside my realm of necessity. Even social pressures became extraneous. I did not like explaining my situation to anyone, so I simply did not see anyone who could possibly need explanation. My rule became 'inner circle only.' The people who had a deep understanding of my situation, and more importantly me, could be trusted with my fragile heart. I said no to baby showers and fundraising events. I said no to any and all social pressures. It was important for me to know what my bandwidth was, so that I could put my inner parts back in their places. That cannot be done while overextending oneself. I chopped my social circle down to an amazing few and they helped me to restore my sense of peace.

The lessons didn't stop there. With the noise of life so incredibly diminished, I began learning the subtext that would become the cornerstone of my healing. Up next, the present moment. Every guru, spiritual teacher, and yoga instructor will preach this same lesson in different ways. Your power resides in the present moment, all other moments do not exist. That's it! I could stop there but I happen to know that more explanation is needed.

Wherever you are on your road of divorce, I can guarantee that it is not easy. The losses are insurmountable, and your ability to manage loss (your partner) is no longer available to you. You have everything to rebuild and your tool box has just gone up in smoke. This is why the present moment is so important. Nobody knows the path to divorce or even next steps. It is basically a mystery to everyone. If your mind is consumed with thoughts of the future, I guarantee you will be drenched in stress. Who the fuck knows what you are supposed to be expecting next week or next year? If your mind is consumed with thoughts from the past, I guarantee you will be drowning in a pool of sadness and regret.

If your thoughts are focused on the present moment, you will be reminded that it is fully handle-able, because, well, it is. Literally any moment that you may find yourself in, you will notice, is fully within your realm of capability. You are an adult with a functioning head on your shoulders. If you dial it into right now, you can proceed to the next moment with a higher sense of confidence knowing that the present moment is all you really need to handle. And here's the best part!!! That thing you are worried about (where am I going to live, will I ever love again, how the fuck do I repair this breaking house?) will also be handled in the present moment—when it gets its turn. When the time comes, you will have more resources, more data, more strength, and more experience to bring a more complete you into the moment of actually making the decision. Trust in yourself, trust in the process, and let that worry go so that it can be solved in the moment that actually owns it.

Do it right now. Look around you. Breath it in and honor it. Focus on your senses and let yourself go deep into the moment. It is from this state of calm that you want to be making decisions anyway. Of course, not all moments are created equal. Have you ever had a client on the phone asking billing questions while changing your baby's diaper, only to discover you have baby poop in your hair? Yep, been there.

So, you may be asking, "What about those moments? What about the times that are truly just fucking stressful? Do I really want to dial into that shit (pun intended)?"

To that I say, which self would you rather bring to the situation? The harried, rushed, judgy self? Or the calmer, deep breathing, knowing it will all work out self? Which self do you think is going to be making the wiser decisions? Those moments are going to come, there is no way around that, but if you hone this skill of staying present minded, you will be amazed at your ability to bring your best self into handling them.

The next question that naturally arises is, "What about those times that I really do need to plan for the future? What about planning my move, or going for a job, or writing a book that I hope to finish? And riddle me this, little miss therapist, if I never think about the past, how can I learn from it? What about the relationship autopsy that you so readily say I need to do while in your cozy office?"

You're going to love the answer to this one because it's so freakin' simple. Just flip it! That's all. Spend the big portion of your time in the present, and the small portion of your time in other places. Anywhere along the divorce train people can get absolutely mired by the "whys" and the "hows." And yes, there is a certain portion of it that certainly needs to happen. But if you typically spend most of your day riddled in thoughts concerning your plight, and that includes talking about it with people, Google searches, and endless mind chatter; and precious few moments in the present, just flip it. There is a time for making your plans. Make them and drop it. There is a time for healing the wounds left by your relationship, work on them and drop it, preferably in your therapist's office. Give yourself time and space for healing and working through it, but keep it contained. Spend the rest of your time living in the present. It doesn't have to be more complex than that.

If you find yourself perseverating in the past or future, tell yourself it's ok, and bring yourself back to the present moment. If you find yourself physically in the shower, but mentally reliving an argument, or going through your laundry list, bring yourself back. This is a great example for bringing yourself back to the moment because there are so many ways to do it. In the shower we are typically alone, we are surrounded by delicious smells, and we are feeling the warm water on our skin. All you have to do is pay attention to the many details that can bring you back to the moment.

Another little secret is that staying present minded is fun. It makes each moment more lively and colorful. It also makes challenges more palatable. One challenge at a time is completely workout-able. This makes things that once seemed ominous more doable. If living in the present can significantly help difficult situations, it can certainly enliven the fun ones. Every moment that you are in will be enhanced by your presence.

As I look back on my time of living as a shell of myself, it was the newly-learned appreciation for staying present minded that really got me through. My life was simply too stressful to take it all on at once. Divorce is actually a great time to work on this skill. Kind of like being chased by wolves is a great time to see how fast you can run. There are some people who do not need a significant event to achieve a new level of enlightenment. Just like there are some people who can become Olympic runners without ever being chased by wild animals. And to those people I say good for you. But for the rest of us, functioning at this level of being, this level of wisdom, takes a significant push. It takes being stripped bare to the bones, hungry, lost, and being chased by wolves to know that there is no turning back. The only way out is through, and the only way through is with presence.

THE SKIN

The skin is an organ too. It is the organ that is all around us and often goes unnoticed as an organ at all. In fact, it's the human body's largest organ. It is the organ that holds the rest of us all together and it's the next one on the coroner's table.

There are certain losses that you will need to feel one at a time. The point to remember here is that you will take each one in and give it the respect that it deserves by both grieving the loss and letting it go. The collateral damage I am referring to here are the people that have nothing to do with your divorce but are hit by the crossfire. You and your ex did not live in a vortex and therefore there are people with whom your relationship will drastically change. Your ex's friends, family members, nieces, and nephews are all victims of this crossfire. These are people who may have once been in your inner circle but because of these circumstances, your engagement with these people will diminish or vanish entirely.

As trite as this may sound, all relationships are destined to change. People come into your life for a period of time, serve a certain purpose, and then life moves on. There may have been a time when you considered these people your family. There may have been a time when these people sprinkled your daily life with birthdays celebrated, holiday traditions, Sunday dinners, nights out, ski weekends, weekend breakfast, pool parties, shared childcare and play dates, weeknight dinners made a bit more festive, work functions, and many more activities that are specific to your life. It is amazing when you think about how much of your time is spent with the people in this circle.

...and it's an extremely bitter pill to swallow when you realize these people are not yours. They came into your life because of your ex and they will exit it to support him or her. That is their place and s/he needs their support. This acknowledgement is practical but it does not make it any easier. These are the people who in one way or another were a part of the fabric of your life. You had years of laughs, tears, spills, and mishaps. You could count on them as family and never thought that there would be a time that they would be considered people in this world that you *used* to know.

In the beginning of a marriage you spend a ton of time cultivating these relationships. For better or for worse, they are a part of the package you signed up for. There are countless horror stories of in-laws, and depending on your situation, these might not be relationships that you will miss. But the difference between ending a marriage and ending a relationship is that when you married your spouse, you married into his family. You took them on as your own.

The longer your marriage, the longer you invest in the growing nature of the family. These people have kids who you also grow to love. You watch as your children form relationships of their own, further grounding your feeling as a solid square in the family quilt. But the truth is they were never fully yours. There are many people who find a way to continue these relationships, especially through children. But for others it is just too hard.

This is a very personal choice. One of my patients spoke so kindly of her ex sister-in-law, and for years was able to maintain that relationship.

"I see how maintaining this relationship is complicated, but I just can't imagine dropping her just because it didn't work out with my ex," she said.

For some, this is a worthy cause. For some, better to try to maintain these relationships knowing that the benefits far outweigh the complications. For me, these relationships were dead on arrival of divorce.

There could be a very palatable difference between those divorcing with kids and those divorcing without. The ones divorcing with children can see those children as reason to keep the relationships alive. It can be seen as a mission to keep Uncle Joe as part of the family, regardless of circumstance. For me it was the opposite. As I have mentioned, when you are stripped bare of all that you are, and you are living in a cocoon, the number of people who receive your energy becomes very limited. I had enough energy to care for myself and my children. The three of us deserved all of it. I no longer had the bandwidth to cultivate relationships outside of the inner core.

Plus, I had too clear of a view of the pitfalls of keeping these relationships alive. For me, the complications were too damaging to risk the homeostasis that I was trying with such fervor to maintain. Simply put, seeing them brought sadness to my heart, and I had no room for any more sadness in my heart. It was too painful to see babies who I knew would not see me as their aunt, but as their dad's brother's ex-wife who hardly comes around anymore. What even is that, anyway? I think of those babies often, and all the nieces, nephews, cousins, and in-laws. They will no longer consider me their family, but as their cousin's mama. It is a loss and they will be terribly missed.

Sometimes "moving on" has such a positive spin to it and other times it is cloaked in the need to let go. I knew before it happened that each of us would move on. Sometimes it helps to see the writing on the wall from the beginning. The collateral damage doesn't garnish the same momentum because there are no hard feelings or tangible reasons for the separation. There was only an unfortunate circumstance that dictated the future of the relationship.

If you are feeling the guilt of keeping these relationships alive, let it go. It is now your ex's responsibility to follow up with birthday parties and Sunday dinners. Your children will still be a part of their lives, but it will be between your ex and his family/friends. They can handle it without you. Your children, if they are of talking age, will report back every detail and keep you informed. You do not need to be the arbiter of these relationships any longer.

However, this hurdle does not come without a silver lining. With the drop in overall familial obligation, there is significantly more time for your circle. That circle will be smaller, but in time you will be able to cultivate stronger relationships by having more energy to dedicate toward them.

One of my recently divorced patients saw the silver lining during his own version of creating space. He was processing every arrow of his divorce right in front of me on his side of the couch. Every Thursday at 9 a.m. he came in with his to-go coffee and short sleeve button down. It could be 40 degrees outside and he would still be in a short sleeve button down. "My arms need to breathe," he would say.

The first few sessions with him always began with him marveling at how long it must have taken me to turn on my office. "You just have so many things going," he would say. "You walk in here and have to turn on the waterfall, the salt lamp, the sound machine, and this misty weird smelling thing."

"It's supposed to be multisensory," I said in return.

"I like it, it's just so many plugs."

Taylor was an electrician and liked to focus on outlets when he didn't know exactly what to say. I usually steered the conversation in accordance with his cadence—small talk, then depth. We would begin with outlets and progress to his divorce. It was a formulaic system to get beyond the surface, which fed into his tendency to be both straight forward and intellectual.

He sipped his coffee with his electrician hands, muscular and slightly callused, but also dexterous from years of working

DIVORCED AS F* IN SEVEN SPIRITUAL STEPS

with small wires. After moving on from the state of my office, we got right down to the meat of his concern. He had been divorced for six months and just started to feel comfortable in his "new life" as he put it. While describing his new hobby of cooking, I asked him how he found the time for it.

"Necessity I guess." Then he continued, "Nah, it's more than that. It started out as just plain hunger. My wife was always the one who did the cooking and I got sick of eating a bowl of cereal every night after we split. At first I figured I would just learn how to cook one dish, so that at least I would have one good meal per week. But then it's like some sort of trance came over me. My house smelled like garlic and I had basil growing right by my kitchen sink. Looking at the basil made me want to learn more about cooking with basil, which in turn made me want to grow more herbs, and so on. I never really thought of it as captivating before, but now I can't stop."

"In my old life" he continued, "I never would have had time to entertain such an idea. We just had so many obligations. There was always a birthday party, a religious gathering, or even a meal that someone else cooked. Don't get me wrong, I loved those things, but it became all encompassing. Now I am more in charge of how I spend my time. I cook my turkey meatballs, and invite only the people who I want to come over. There are no obligatory invites because my obligations were literally cut in half."

"Sounds so freeing," I said back. "I know that time spent alone has been difficult for you, and this seems to have filled that space."

"Yeah it did, but in a way that feels preordained. It was actually more freeing to be happy with a bowl of cereal. Actually, nothing is quite that freeing. That's like living in a world with a very low sense of adulting. I could just have a low maintenance meal and be done with it. But now something has taken its place and it needed time in order to cultivate and grow. I can't go back to that bowl of cereal now. There are just too many flavors out there and I won't be satisfied unless I am reaching for all of them. When I sit down to a good meal, it's so much more satisfying, and I'm willing to put in the time to make it happen. I don't know, when I was caught in the place of obligation, it just wasn't as important to me to make it happen. I didn't have time. Now I have Taco Tuesday with friends and it's one of the things I look forward to most each week."

"What is different about having people over before and having people over now?"

"That's the beauty of it," he continued. "It's practically the same thing, except now each person who comes over is there by choice. There is not one person dragged by that feeling of duty. It changes the composition of the night and brings with it a sense of fun. Don't get me wrong, I'm a family guy and love spending time with family, but I'm starting to think that one family truly is plenty. My family plus her family led to a ridiculous amount of required attendance."

"It seems like it's not just about one thing, but about the culmination of many."

"Right, and how could I not appreciate that?"

"This is about more than just need," I said. "It's about the stretch. You had to stretch yourself to meet the demands of your new life. 'The Chef' was inside you somewhere. He was always there. But in order for him to emerge, you had to get seriously sick of eating Fruity Pebbles. The excess time gave you the opportunity to indulge in that wanting. Sometimes longing for something can be a very tangible motivator."

"Yeah exactly! I never would have predicted this a few months ago. Back then all I could see was an overwhelming sadness. But now I see things starting to come together. I still feel the sadness, but it's dispersed by these times when I can let myself emerge."

Taylor continued to feel 'the stretch' in many ways. He had a long road in dealing with a very complicated and messy divorce. The saying 'Death by a thousand cuts' pertains to the small losses that seemingly come out of nowhere, but just keep coming. Divorce can bring many of those. The skin is an organ that protects us from the harshness of the outside world. When the skin gets cut, it is just as important to acknowledge that impact as we would for the rest of our organs. As is acknowledging the impact of collateral damage. If these losses are given their space and time to heal, there will be no death at all. Only strategically placed bandages all over a healing person. Along Taylor's road, we kept honoring the impact by pointing out aspects of his journey that never would have coalesced if he were stuck in old patterns. He felt the loss, created space for the new, and then dedicated time so that the new would have a fighting chance. His sessions with me helped him to bring awareness to those moments as they happened so that he could feel a sense of ownership over them. This was healing. This was growth.

Relationship Autopsy In Summation

- Game day replay. Take a moment to look at what worked and what didn't.

- Did your body send you messages at any point during the relationship, and did you listen? Identifying these signals will help you to be more aware of them in future.

- Use the pain of the situation to stay present minded.

- Know that divorce brings collateral damage but be mindful of the silver linings as well.

CHAPTER FOUR

ACCEPTANCE

POOL OF NEUTRALITY

"For after all, the best thing one can do when it is raining is let it rain." - Henry Wadsworth Longfellow

On a hot summer day sometime in the mid-80s, I gathered my Punky Brewster towel and flip flops and headed outside to the front yard of my childhood home. With anticipation, I waited for my mom, sister, and brother to come out after me and hop into the car. I was dressed in nothing more than a bathing suit and goggles, and sat among the caterpillars as I thought about how that was the day I was going to perfect my underwater handstand. Kai and I had already developed a very intricate rating system on the ultimate synchronized swimming move, and I was sure my new technique would give me the boost in ratings to score the championship. All I needed to do was point my toes and bend at the knees to the beat of the latest Debbie Gibson song. Then hold the posture for as long as the lungs could withstand and come up for air. It was a winning combination and sure to impress.

My mother and siblings walked out the door holding a gargantuan cooler filled with lunch goodness, and called for me to put the caterpillar down and hop into the car. It was officially community pool time.

Sandwiched in-between my brother and sister in the dreaded middle seat, I took my place at the bottom of the sibling seating arrangement totem pole. There was a seating hierarchy that could only be achieved with age and I knew my place. I didn't like it, but also didn't care enough to cause a scene. I had much bigger fish to fry in the four-foot big kid section of the community pool.

My mom turned the key and we heard a strange popping noise blast out the back of the station wagon, and then silence. Where was the hum of the engine turning over? Where was the sound of my mom's continuous classical music blasting through the one front speaker? For reasons unknown, the car just didn't work. In the mind of a seven-year-old, there were cars that worked, and those that didn't. All I knew was that I was buckled into the middle of a brown car with bucket seats that didn't work. That meant no pool, no handstand championship, and absolutely no alternatives. There were no other kids on our street and I had already played in the sprinkler six times that day. The disappointment was palpable, and the heat of the day was exacerbated by the realization of no pool time. *Why me*, I thought, *of all days?*

"Well kids, praise the Lord for everything. Let's put those sandwiches back in the fridge," my mom said nonchalantly with a shrug.

What? I thought. *Praise the lord for everything? What is that Mom? I don't want to praise anyone for anything right now. I want to go to the pool and demonstrate the crap out of my handstand abilities. Now I'm stuck here with nothing to do and a mother preoccupied with fixing a car!*

Punky power was not going to get me out of this one. I sulked and I fell on the grass out of sheer boredom. With the trees above me and the smell of honeysuckle all around me, I thought about how it was possible for my mother to praise such a moment. What was she thinking and why does she always say that? Don't certain moments just suck? Can't we just say that this blows and I'm sorry that we all have to go through it? This may have been the first time in my life that I found myself diametrically and unequivocally opposed to the opinion of an adult. "Sorry Mom," I wanted to say, "I'm not buying it."

I don't know what got me off the grass that day. It was probably hunger—it always seems to be hunger. I sat down in the kitchen and looked up at my mom with sad eyes and a growling belly. I started to peel a banana when she said, "I know you're disappointed, honey. As soon as the car is fixed we can go to the pool."

"But then why, Mom? Why do you say 'praise the Lord for everything'? Even when we are stuck in this house with no air conditioning and no pool?"

"Because we have no way of knowing what His plans are. Maybe He could see that we were headed for an accident, and then guided the winds that guided our car to break, thereby averting the accident altogether. Or maybe it's none of that. Maybe there is a lesson in here that each one of us needs to learn in our own way. The point is that I don't really know sweetie. What I do know is that I have faith in His plan. I praise Him for all that comes in my path because I know that it is all a part of His plan."

What I could have said at that time was "Wow Mom, sounds a bit meaty for a seven-year-old." But that was not my reaction at all. I took it in. I absorbed it to the bone. It would take decades to grapple with the idea of divine intervention and Godly overreach, because that never really sat well with me for various reasons, but I could not help but agree that the sentiment started a shift in my thinking and in my day. I started thinking of the hypothetical accident that could have left us stranded on the side of the road, or much worse. Suddenly, taking out my set of paints to sketch yet another horse painting didn't sound so bad. I started thinking of all the creature comforts I was so happy to have that wouldn't have been available to me if I were stuck somewhere on Jericho Turnpike.

My siblings and I have often joked about my mom's proclivity for Jesus. Whenever she talks in parables, we refer to Jesus as her boyfriend. She has always seemed so lucky in love, so starry-eyed surprise, when talking about Jesus that we could come to no other conclusion. She clearly has a

Christian perspective that is so pure, so undeniable, that it would be nearly impossible to not pick up some of her effervescent glow in regard to Him. However, what I picked up on that day was not so much of a strong religiosity or love for the Big Man, but more of a change in perspective.

I felt in one minute how my mood was glum, negative, and infused with 'poor-me'; and in the next minute my mood turned to be more thankful and appreciative. What my mother gave me that day was the ability to shift my mood based upon a shift in perspective. She did it in real time, using real situations.

I could see that at the ripe age of 7, but what would take an additional 33 years to figure out was the way in which she did it. Because before we can "praise the Lord for everything," or shift perspective, or see the light among darkness, we must first accept what is. What she did not do was bang her head against the steering wheel and start blaming outside forces. Nor did she show any signs of hopelessness or even fatigue. Her first action was to accept what is. "Oh well kids" means, in translated Mom speak, "this is our situation now and it's up to us to deal with it."

Her speed to acceptance is unprecedented. Most of us would need at least a few moments to throw out a few expletives. Fuck, I can't go one chapter without venting frustration in one way or another. So, the point here is not to feel less than because the rest of us are not on her level of Zen mastery, but more to show the point that there is a process. And that process begins with acceptance. First, she accepted the situation for what it was. There was no changing it and therefore out of her control.

I immediately saw this situation as bad. She did not. She saw it as neutral. And herein lies the sweet grand lesson. Situations are neither good nor bad. They simply are what they are. Or to quote basically everyone I have ever met in my life "it is what it is." How many fucking times have I heard that quote without fully absorbing it? Oh great, another person reminding me that it is what it is. Thanks to the sagacious public for making that one feel like wallpaper. However, it can't be denied that they might be onto something.

The truth is, and I'm dropping some real shit here, when a situation arises it does not fall neatly into the good bucket or bad bucket. There are not good eggs and bad eggs when it comes to life experiences. Some seemingly bad situations may be the catalyst that brings you to spiritual enlightenment, in which case how could you possibly call it bad? There are also those classic lottery winner situations in which the person becomes miserable, and missing the old, less complicated life.

So, if the situation isn't what makes the outlook good or bad, then what is? How do we define shit show versus funky town? DMV versus hip parade? The answer circles right back to neutrality. The situation is always neutral. Every single one. They are all right smack in the middle of good or bad because they are neither. Losing your job, neutral. Car breaking down, neutral. And yep, you guessed it. Divorce—neutral.

To demonstrate, think back to the movie *Sliding Doors* with Gwyneth Paltrow. When the main character, Helen, is fired from her job and rushes out to catch a train, two scenarios take place. In one, she gets on the train and comes home to find her boyfriend, Gerry (John Lynch), cheating on her. In the second, she misses the train and arrives after the other woman has left. In the first scenario, Helen, having experienced a clear deal breaker, dumps Gerry, and moves on with her life. In the second, she becomes increasingly unhappy because of a constant suspicion of Gerry's infidelity. The film continues to alternate between the two storylines in which different events ensue.

There are so many points to unpack from this movie, but let's stick with the degree of fortunate versus unfortunate nature of the events. During moments like missing a train, many would quickly conclude that it is an unfortunate circumstance. She ran, she tried hard to catch it, she dropped an earring, and she missed it. She clearly wanted to catch the train, but because of circumstance, she did not get what she wanted. Not getting what one wants is often viewed as negative or unfortunate. Especially in our society where there is such a strong emphasis placed on getting what one wants.

However, it was this circumstance that teased life to display the truth of her relationship. So, could she then conclude that missing the train that day was a fortunate event? The truth is, there was no way for her to know how that was going to play out. It tripped a series of events in her life that she never could have predicted. So if there were any feelings of dissent regarding missing the train, they turned out to be erroneous. If we cannot predict the outcome of any event, how can we place a positive or negative value on it?

Then there was the scene of catching her boyfriend in bed with another woman. Would she have preferred to stay in darkness? Maybe discovering the truth was not what she wanted. Many would go to great lengths to discover the truth. That was the reason why private investigators were invented. She discovered the truth in a punch-to-the gut type of way. Some people would want to protect themselves from such a jarring event. While perhaps others would think of it as the catalyst that launched her into a swift and formidable change.

The positive and negative attributes associated with each circumstance change like the wind depending on perspective. Even perspective changes as time continues and more future moments are revealed. The only true constant is the event itself. The event, without judgment, without thought, and without emotional reaction, simply just exists. It is what it is. Those fuckers were right.

In both the movie and in life, the aspect that turns a situation to the proverbial dark side is your thoughts surrounding it. If you miss a train and your thoughts include "Why me? Why do I have such bad luck?" of course your mood will turn sour. If you think about the car breaking down as the penultimate to social-life disaster, then your mood will follow and so will the rest of your thoughts. However, if you see either one of these situations as your next hurdle, during a life full of hurdles, that will inevitably teach you the next lesson in your soul's journey, then we are headed into herculean personal growth.

By quietly observing the thoughts as an entity other than yourself, you give them less power. Actually, you take away their power completely and create space to proactively choose thoughts that will benefit you.

My patients often ask "But HOW? Really, how am I supposed to just choose one thought over another? They just happen!"

To that question, I set them up with a story. I tell them that a meteor is about to hit the office, and then wait patiently as they do nothing. I tell them again that the meteor is gaining speed and heading straight for the window. Since they continue to do nothing, I ask them why they are just sitting there and not running out of the building. They say, quite matter-of-factly, that they don't believe me. They remained seated because they were not convinced, and therefore the words had no emotional impact. Therefore, there was no panic, no increased heart rate, no thoughts of doom, and no legs moving at lightning speed.

I then point out to them that the thought of a meteor was put into their head, and was of no consequence because there was no BELIEF in it. The essential difference is that thoughts can come and go as they please, but if you do not believe in them, they hold no power. It is not the thought itself, but your belief in the thought that causes an emotional reaction. This is one of the cornerstones of Cognitive Behavioral Therapy. Therefore, do not push thoughts away. Let them come and let them go. The ones that hold negativity can be disputed as irrational and the rest can float in and float out. This is how you observe your thoughts, and then make a conscious decision to act or not act upon them. You can make a conscious decision to choose the good ones.

Your awareness of your thoughts will help you to lead them. I have spoken before about the separation between you and your thoughts. You are not your thoughts. Therefore, when they become dark, when Darth Vader seems to take over and predict nothing good, you can identify Darth Vader as the Sith that he is, watch him walk in, and watch him walk out. You don't have to judge him or curse his arrival. He is a dark lord who wants attention, but you know how to direct him and his loud breathing apparatus directly out the door by refocusing your attention on your inner stillness. You don't have to become Darth just because he entered your purview, just as you don't have to become your dark thoughts just because they entered your brain.

Could you imagine if Darth walked into a room and no one gave a shit? His bravado would melt away under a black cape, and he would walk out the door in search of other creatures to scare. Because really, Darth is a toddler. He wants attention and pitches a fit if he doesn't get it. Our dark thoughts are no different. They are the low frequency, immature, undeveloped thoughts that seek attention only to disturb. You have the choice to cultivate these thoughts and thereby stay in this frame of reference, or not. You also have a choice to recognize that cultivating low frequency thoughts will only lead you in a direction that is unrecognizable to your true character.

The other thoughts, the positive, self-empowering thoughts that own the shit out the present moment will be the ones that help your true self to shine. And as we all know, thoughts become things, so the thoughts that you cultivate will turn into the behaviors that emanate from you naturally. I often tell my patients that you know you are on the right track when your actions are in line with your intentions. Meaning, when you say you want to play the piano, and then you dedicate time toward playing the piano, your intentions and your behaviors are in perfect alignment.

So, if you keep saying that you just want to move on from your past relationship, but your thoughts continue to circle around your ex and his/her whereabouts, then you are not harmonious with your intentions. You are not lined up. The way through this is just to be aware of your thoughts. The dark ones will not cease immediately, but they will have significantly less power when you label them, and let them walk out the door like a deflated Darth Vader.

So, in both missed trains and missed days at the pool, the big chunks and the little chunks, it turns out that my mother was right. Maybe not about the averted accident part, that I will never know, but the lesson I learned that day taught me far more than an easy day at the pool ever could have. I watched her as she remained neutral about the reality of the situation, she chose the thoughts that helped her to stay positive, and her actions were in line with her intentions. She helped me to learn that perspective has a tangible effect on mood, behavioral outcomes, and depth of character. That is quite enough for a kid. But as an adult, the next big lesson is that it applies to the big chunks as well. When all situations are kept in neutrality, including job loss, heart break, divorce, panic attacks, etc., we have far greater power to choose the outcome. Will this stinking turd of a stumbling block on life's journey cause you to get stuck in a rut, or will it be the catalyst to a higher plain? The choice, truly, is yours.

Bringing Neutral Home

Ok, ok, so we have a choice in how to view things. But what about the other side of it? What about how difficult this is for the kids? What about the years of pain and stress associated with divorce? How on earth could this bring about anything but a muted version of all I used to have?

Because there is growth in pain. However, I will not deny that it hurts. Different aspects hurt at different times. What hurts the most for me now is to see the pain in my daughter's eyes. I can't deny it when she comes to me with pain in her heart and tears in her eyes and says, "But why Mama? Why can't he just live with us again? It's so hard to separate our time with him and our time with you." I tell her that if I could take the pain from her heart and put it into mine, I would, but I can't. All I can do is give her all of me, all of my presence, to sit with her in her sadness for as long as she needs me to (her mom is a therapist after all). I sit with her pain because there is no sugar coating it. It is real and it is hard and there is nothing I can say that will make it go away. She will have struggles that I never had as a kid. Of course I want to protect her from them and keep her in a bubble. But instead, I hold her hand, absorb her tears, and show her an example of compassion that she can keep with her always.

So yes it hurts. I wish I could take it away for you as well, and everyone who comes into my office, but I can't. So instead, I write words that will show you how there is growth in your pain. It doesn't come all at once, but with awareness it comes and it heals. As you are feeling the suffering, your spirit is growing in ways you never could have imagined. You are detaching yourself from what you once thought made you who you are. As you strip yourself of your ego attachments, you are coming closer to the truest version of yourself. The part of you that has always been there, before your marriage, before your adulthood, before you were born. That intrinsic part of you that seeks to experience and understand and grow. With every tear shed, with every sleepless night, you are breaking through walls built through the years. The death of one brings the birth of another. We see this in the wild all the time. The snake must shed its skin, the butterfly must shed its cocoon, and so on. As humans, we want the fresh new skin and the butterfly wings without experiencing the pain of it. Not only that, but we want it now.

This is where addiction loves to slip in. Because of our human propensity for instant pain gratification, we often turn to a drug to slip right in and ease our pain with immediateness and swiftness. I guarantee that this will give you a hangover and will postpone the inevitable. But that is not what I am trying to stress here. I want you to raise your awareness to this truth. Drugs/alcohol postpone, while feeling deeply and with distance will eventually lesson the pain. You will need the formula of time, plus concerted effort, equals moving through it. $T + E = M$. This formula may not be my most eloquent moment, but it is one that needs to be imprinted on the side of your skull.

Every person who is in therapeutic treatment is experiencing $T + E = M$. Time is the denominator and is going by anyway. That is the part that you cannot control. Time alone does not necessarily promote growth because living some version of the same day over and over will only bring on more of the same. When time continues in this way without growth, people tend to say they are stuck in a rut, or not feeling engaged.

The effort is what changes things. Effort can come in the form of therapy, changing perspective, learning new ways to handle things, changing the status quo, changing your environment, or reading books. Effort often starts with curiosity, and continues with action. "I wonder if starting therapy might help me handle all that is going on," one might say. Then shortly after, that person calls a few therapists to begin the process. Someone could be curious about psychotropic medication, and the action that needs to follow is calling a psychiatrist. "I wonder if I could get back involved with my kickball team," could pop into one's mind. That is great, follow up with a call and a calendar invite. Effort, by definition, means trying, and you can try at anything. Some aspects of what you try may not be fitting for you right now. That is ok. Keep trying anyway. Eventually something will stick.

But still, you may wonder, I was growing before this bullshit. I was learning and expanding and maturing as a person. Why did I need a swift kick in the ass to experience the benefits?

Yes. There are some people in this world who are able to grow without suffering, and that is amazing and admirable. They usually come in the form of monks and have an unending amount of time to put toward spiritual growth. I don't see that as particularly helpful for people in our situation. We need to live in this world and we don't have that kind of time.

Before this point, you had no reason to break down your ego. Why would you when you could skip along under the guise that you were your role. Your role as spouse or parent was your identity, so you could focus on being the best of those two things. However, separation from these two things brings a wisdom that actually helps you become better at them. When you learn to focus on your being, stripped of its roles, you learn to become vested in the present moment.

It is this awareness of the present that teaches you to be fully with the being in front of you. I have seen my children benefit from this awareness. When I am with them, I am fully with them, in a way that I never was before. My clients reap the benefits of a more evolved therapist on the other side of the couch. Every one of my roles has been enhanced because of this situation. I tell you this not to brag but to assure you that these benefits are waiting for you as well.

When my patient, Taylor, became involved with cooking, it changed his approach to not only food but to every aspect of his life. He shared his curiosity for cooking with his kids as they watched the herbs grow, and with his friends as they all shared a meal together. He brought those around him into the moment by sharing his appreciation of it. He challenged himself to come into presence, and experienced personal growth as a result. This is a small example of big change. Something in him needed to break down in order for something else to break through. The crisis in his life created space, and effort from him let the connectedness emerge. His talent, his curiosity, his pure love for cooking was already there, and Time, plus Effort, helped him to Move into his new way of being.

Challenges are not seen as negative in the spiritual world. They are a part of the journey that will help you to connect to your inner self. Your job then is to be aware of their essential role in bringing you to where you need to be. Your job is to shift perspective and own both the ups and the downs. One is dependent on the other. Your marriage is gone, your ego is in question, your false vision of the future has evaporated. And with that void comes a powerful and impactful starting point. Once you are stripped down, you will value what is left tenfold because it is your being. It is the core of you unattached to your roles. Sounds selfish, but it couldn't be further from it. When you are with a person, you will do nothing but be with that person. When you are collecting seashells, you will do nothing but collect seashells. That is how you will connect to yourself and others. It is the greatest gift you can give. How on earth was the biggest challenge of your life once seen as bad? Hard, yes. Difficult, absolutely. But you will move through it while experiencing the benefits of your effort.

CHOSEN WEEKEND

One rainy Thursday morning in spring I walked into Bettie's office feeling like I had turned a corner. It had been a few months of therapeutic crying and trying to understand it all, but on that day I felt like I had a new message to tell her. She had helped me through so many of the questions, but this time I felt like I had more of the answers to share. I sat in her cozy waiting room, sinking into the couch cushions from heaven, and breathing in the citrus aromatherapy. The windchime CD was playing on repeat and inviting me to feel the calm. She opened the door and gestured toward her space of emotional healing.

I sat down in my spot, the same spot that knew about my innermost thoughts for over a decade. The same spot where I breastfed my babies when I couldn't get a sitter for my session. The same spot that held my tears and rejoiced in my affirmations. The same spot that knew the rise and fall of my marriage, and every painstaking emotion that went along with it.

Her first question came out so quickly it was like she had been waiting all day to ask it. "So how was it?!"

I had told her in a session prior that my girlfriends and I had planned a long weekend away. It was a way to celebrate our collective 40th birthdays, and also a way to celebrate a long and beautiful friendship between four women.

"It was really great," I said, "so great in fact that I wish I could relive it a million times over."

"That's amazing, you look so happy!"

"I feel it for sure. It was the culmination of so much really. It's been a tough few months and it felt so good to be untethered with such great friends. There was this moment on the beach when Ellie and I started dancing just like we used to in high school. The music was playing from a little speaker on our beach chairs, and we had a glass of white in our hands. We jumped right into this dance that embodies a weird combination of MC Hammer and freestyle. Our friends Rachel and Skylar, being products of the 90s themselves, joined right in. The four of us were dancing and singing our hearts out on a sunny, windy beach as if nothing else existed. And what's crazy is that in a way, nothing else did. We all had kids and jobs and responsibilities at home, but that moment was about us." My mouth began to contort into a silent chuckle as I said, "The funniest part is that it continued every day we were there. Each destination brought a new dance and a new reason to get lost in the moment. While we were hanging out by the pool, we were dancing, waiting for the elevator, dancing, out on the balcony, dancing. My strappy wedge heels have never seen so much action."

I looked away with a far off smile that happens when people are recounting a wonderful memory. When I looked back at Bettie, I couldn't believe what I saw. Tears. Actual, beautiful, happy tears.

With her fingers just slightly brought to her chin she said, "You're going to be ok. With everything you have been through, this is living, breathing proof that you are going to be ok. I had faith that you would, and it just makes me so happy to see it on your face."

"Wow, you really do care!" I said in flattered astonishment.

Good therapists really do care. We carry your stories with us in a protective space in our minds. When you are sitting in front of us there is nothing but you and the interaction that reverberates in the air. Bettie, in particular, epitomized caring.

"Of course I do," she said. "But how did you do it? I mean really. I know that you have had many difficult times over the past few months, but how were you able to put them aside and enjoy your friends?"

Her question made me think of the corner I had been turning in just those few weeks, and how for this session I had more answers than questions. I wanted to show her the progress I had been making.

"Because I finally owned it. I realized that I chose all of it. I chose this place in life and I need to choose how to handle it."

"So in the past you would say that he was making the wrong decision by leaving, but you are now saying that on some level you wanted it as well?"

"No, I don't mean that I wanted this. I never did and I still don't. I mean that I need to live each moment AS IF I chose it. Don't mind my quoting iconic 90s movies, but it really is AS IF all moments have a lesson to teach." I thought about my mother and her 'praise the Lord' mumbo jumbo. "Someone cuts you off in line, you chose it because it taught you patience, someone was rude to you, you chose it because it taught you to stand up for yourself, someone stole something from your basement, you chose it because it taught you to protect yourself."

"So by 'owning it' you are saying you see the lesson in it... the spiritual growth," she said, eloquently surmising weeks of realizations and epiphanies.

"Fuck yeah," I replied, having long since dropped curbing my F bombs. "I may not have wanted a divorce or anything that goes along with it, but I wouldn't change anything along my path. Each hurdle of bullshit had key significance to my spiritual unfolding. I once argued with you that I didn't need bullshit in order to grow. I thought I could grow just fine by taking classes and the like. Remember that?"

"Of course," she said.

"You said that sometimes it just does. It takes something big. Well, I have had something big. And now I see what you were saying more clearly. I chose to emerge from quite possibly the darkest time in my life by going on a girls weekend with friends that I love. I knew that we would laugh and celebrate in a beautiful setting. I was able to absorb that for the joy that it was. Days like that are undeniably blissful and I wasn't going to miss out on it just because of days of pain."

I continued on with my diatribe, "I also knew that I could break down because, ya know, I still miss him as fucked up as that is. There were moments when I really felt the pain of loss. But it was ok because I was surrounded by supportive people who helped me through that as well."

"This is so good, and it's not fucked up, Bern. That is grieving and you are allowed to feel it," she said.

"It is, Bettie, it is," I continued, loving the fact that I had a listening ear to my most recent rants. "On some level I chose all of this. I chose to be married to someone who has a very different personality than mine. I chose to try hard at something because I believed it to be the right path at the time. But that time has changed and clinging to it was doing me no good. Acceptance has its benefits. It's freeing, really. It's no longer something that happened to me. It just is what it is and now I feel the impact of personal growth in everything that I do."

"Everything? Really?"

"Well, not everything," I said ready for a new topic. "I'm going out on my first real post-divorce date tomorrow night and I'm freaking out a little."

I spent the rest of the session talking about the prospect of dating again. I figured that there were times for talking about the unbearable weightlessness of spiritual growth, and there were times to talk about what to wear on a first date. Turns out I desperately needed a bit of both. Balance, Bettie, it's all about balance.

Acceptance In Summation

- Learn how to see situations as neutral, and thereby own your reactions to them.

- There will be growth in your pain when you apply effort.

- You chose every moment in your life. Even if you didn't, live as if you did.

CHAPTER FIVE

MOVING ON

INTRO TO MOVING ON

Timing is everything and nothing in the divorce world. It means so much, but it will never be perfect. Keep in mind that you are a port in the storm for someone else, and vice versa. This dynamic didn't exist in the pre-divorce dating world. Now, your world has been blown up and so has his. The only difference is the timing of the wreckage. How long ago did your world blow up, and how does that translate to your readiness to be in a new relationship? This is said with the admonition that it is one thing to begin dating, and entirely something else to start a relationship. Beginning a relationship is highly contingent on how far past the wreckage you are. If you are in the eye of the storm, it will be very hard to have the focus and selflessness that a relationship requires. There are so many mitigating factors to a person's timeline for feeling ready, but a rather accurate barometer is in how long you have been separated. It's kind of like judging a person's maturation by his or her age. Age is not a perfect indicator of maturity, but in most circumstances it gets the job done.

Consider this when deciding to date, and deciding who you are going to date. If you are dating someone who just separated from his or her partner one month prior, you are opening yourself up to many risk factors. Including but not limited to, is there a chance for reconciliation? Will this person need to move? Will this person be able to handle the stress that is surely coming down the pike? Are you willing to be a possible escape route? Will you be falling for someone who is consciously or subconsciously using you to weather the storm? There are many pitfalls to unearth and we will discuss them in the chapters that follow.

Your readiness to begin a relationship rests in a place that only you can see. Your readiness to move on begins at the moment of separation and has nothing to do with dating. Moving on comes from the place where you channel your effort. As previously discussed, Time plus Effort equals Moving on. Therefore, channel your effort into something that you find to be positive, and you will experience the benefits of moving on. In this chapter, I will focus on dating because it comes with many inherent challenges. If you decide to join that kickball league, that is amazing, but the details therein do not need to be worked through. Go and have fun. If you decide to focus your effort on dating, it is important to be smart about it so that you can enjoy the ride.

THE COMFORT POTENTIAL RATIO:
DEGREES FROM NETFLIX

The decision to begin dating again after divorce is always a decision. It is not something that just happens to you or falls upon you. This decision could begin with that chance encounter at the coffee shop, or with a deliberate effort to create a profile on a dating app. Either way, you have sent a clear message to the universe that you are back on the market, ready or not. There is no formula for such a personal choice. Some will be ready straight away, some will need more time. There is simply no right answer, so I am not going to pretend to have the magical advice that will enlighten you to when it is your day to begin. Instead, I will bring your awareness to what I call the comfort potential ratio.

There are certain situations that clearly imbibe a significantly increased propensity for comfort. For all intents and purposes, let's use Netflix as the ground zero for personal comfort. You have a remote in your hand, a cozy blanket, and most likely your own home. This is a relaxing, non-threatening, pleasurable way to spend your time. Taking that leap into dating post-divorce is inherently taking a giant leap out of your comfort zone. It is nowhere near the ground zero of Netflix comfort. However, the person you choose to go on that date with will strongly take you varying degrees away from Netflix.

In the beginning, you can choose to go only one degree away from Netflix by choosing someone you already know. This can be someone from the office, a friend, or an ex from your past. This category of potential dates is safely placed in the comfort cohort because there is a plethora of information of which you are already privy. You know who this person is, and, more importantly, who this person is not. There is significantly less potential for scary surprises with this category which is relatively comforting and offers a more relaxed approach to "getting your feet wet."

The burden you must take on with this cohort is the awareness of diminished potential. Having already known this person, you can ease your mind of thoughts of date rape and ax murderers. The reason for diminished potential is the same as the reason for comfort. If you already know them, and they have been in your life in one capacity or another, why hasn't the spark already happened? Why hasn't that line of fate already been tripped up? Of course your circumstance was different, but even within that construct, if there were any spark at all, this category of people would have been placed in the marital danger zone and you would have known it. All other people from this cohort have very low potential for spark. Whether you like it or not, they have already been placed in the friend zone for good reason and it is very difficult to take that leap into the relationship zone.

That is not to say that this cohort should be skipped. Much to the contrary. This is a perfect place to begin dating after divorce because, quite bluntly, you have enough on your mind and you just don't need to add date rape to your litany of concerns. Go out and have some dinner and adult conversation. But your awareness of the comfort potential ratio will keep you from getting disappointed when the relationship fizzles out. It's not your fault; you were just too comfortable.

As you turn the tides of the comfort potential ratio, you will find yourself in a new place. Simultaneously, you are ready to take on more risk, yet still holding on to the need for a dating security blanket. This translates into a date in the form of a friend of a friend. You don't know this person, which is scary, but you know someone who does. There is solace therein for many reasons, and little reason not to go down this path. The potential is high but the list is short. At first, your friends and family will want to set you up on these dates, but you only have so many friends, and they have even less single friends. You will burn through this list in a hot minute and eventually get to a place where you want to have more control over who you date.

If you have found an actual relationship from the above two categories, then good for you. You do not need to continue reading this chapter. If not, then you know you will need to dive into the next cohort. This is the one placed at a full ten degrees from Netflix. You need to be fully ready and fully prepared because this cohort has a small filtering system and is otherwise known as internet dating. Scary at first because you don't know this person, the internet doesn't even know this person. This opens you up to a long list of nefarious situations including cat fishing, roofies, ghosting, and much more. But this also opens you up to endless potential! The dates in this cohort come with a very low degree of comfort, and an extremely high degree of potential. The fact that you have never met this person can be a huge bonus. You are in a stage of new beginnings and this is a chance to indulge in the pleasures of that freedom. This has new chapter written all over it, and there has not been a time in your life when new chapters could be more welcome. Take it, run with it, and go someplace public with a clearly-defined exit strategy.

It is your journey, so you can begin your return to dating with any degree from Netflix as you choose. Some will need to begin with comfort, some will be able to jump right in and not look back. The important part is your awareness of your needs at any given time. You can go back and forth on this continuum as your needs change. The question you will ask yourself is, how many degrees from Netflix would I like to be at this given point? Adjust your comfort potential ratio accordingly and with awareness. Continue questioning what worked for you and why. There is just as much to be ascertained from the dates that did not go well as the ones that did. As you continue to question, you will come upon more clarity as to what you are really looking for. Every time you put yourself out there, it is a success because you learned something about yourself. If you are ready for it, this is a great bucket in which to focus energy.

THE GREAT TRANSITION

I mentioned that there are pitfalls to dating. Let's take a deeper look into them so that you can build a resilience to the turbulence you may experience. I have heard from many patients, and experienced it myself, that beginning dating after divorce feels like entering a world that has moved on without you. It feels foreign and rusty and thrilling and confusing. One minute you are meeting your husband on the couch for a snuggle and a movie after the two of you put your children to bed. The next minute you are sitting at a bar hoping to God your internet date doesn't ghost you, leaving you with a large babysitter bill and pit in your stomach.

Most of us have not been on the dating scene for many years, if not decades. The game has completely changed and so have the rules. Whatever the emotion that accompanies you to the gates of the dating scene, I can assure you are normal. But in this torrent of varied emotion, there is a safe harbor of calm that will get you through it all. Beneath all the thoughts that attempt to ascribe judgments and labels to a situation is a deep knowing that really all this is, is a conversation. It's truly that simple. No pretense, no judgments, and no timetable. It is just two adults committing to each other for one conversation. If that conversation goes well, there will be another one. If it doesn't, the two will part and wish each other luck. When this situation is broken down to its purest form, it becomes significantly less daunting, and surprisingly more fun.

Now that we have stripped the dating scene into the most basic of human interactions, we can proceed with the details of how to make this happen online, otherwise known as a full ten degrees from Netflix. There are a few hallmark differences between dating for the general population and dating in the divorce world. These differences need to be let loose so that you can feel well informed and therefore confident. One key difference is that our people have been through a shit storm. Regardless of the circumstances of your divorce, you have been through the ringer in terms of complete and total life upheaval. You may be completely fine at the moment of dating contact, but your not too distant past is riddled with some serious sleepless nights and utter exhaustion. As a result, your bullshit meter is sensitive. You do not have time for someone who says one thing but means another. Which brings me to my first bullet point.

1. Know your place. Are you looking for a relationship? Are you looking for a hookup? Are you looking for companionship that leads nowhere but is enjoyable for the moment? These are all honorable pursuits and I urge you to proceed with all of them without judgment. But be clear on where you stand, and don't be afraid to make your position known. Whatever your stance, own it because the people who are looking for more or less do not want to waste their precious time and babysitting money on someone who has clearly different goals. You can state your intentions quite clearly using internet dating speech such as LTR (long term relationship), JL (just looking), or LDR (long distance relationship), among many others.

2. Your profile. I will keep this short and simple because it is so personal. So I will just say... keep it real. Show pics that really look like you; you on a good day, but you. Show your fun side, in whatever way that translates best. If you like to travel, show it. If you ride bicycles, snap a pic of you with your bike. People respond to personality equally as much as high cheekbones. In the post-divorce world, mentions of your scene are critical! Let it be known if you have kids and don't

want more, or have kids and want more, etc. This is a key point in the culling process, and if you are looking to save time, know what you have and what you are looking for in regard to family progression.

3. Meet up as soon as possible. This may seem obvious, but it is far too easy to get caught up in the mire of texting and talking. Before you meet the jokes may fly easily, and the person may seem ultra-relatable, but trust me when I say you are playing with fire. So much can be ascertained with a face-to-face meeting, and before this happens you simply have no idea whether or not this person is worth your time. Even if the texts make you laugh and the conversations are thrilling, you do not have expendable time and energy to waste on a person you have not met. Take the relationship out of the phone and meet up for coffee, a walk in the park, or a drink. It doesn't really matter, just stop investing in a fantasy. You are too good for that type of mismanagement.

4. Go in with an out. Since essentially what you are investing in is a face-to-face conversation, there's no reason to sign yourself up for a marathon. A full day plan is a mistake. Keep the initial commitment short and let the rule of simple conversations take effect. If a transition from a coffee to a full dinner is excitingly warranted, let the universe pull you in that direction. If it does, the night will spontaneously unfold as hunger pangs and a thirst for more of those lovely conversations guide the two of you to your next venture. When you go in with an out, you can rest on the confidence that you will have a wonderful night regardless of this unknown person. You will either fully enjoy your date for however long it lasts, or you will leave after one drink and hop right into your backup plan. This can be anything from meeting up with friends or heading to a bookstore. Either way, you got this.

The general theme to online dating is to tangibly remember that there is nothing more precious than your time. The second you notice yourself veering from that feeling of being all in, break away. You will know you are here when you feel like you are compromising or trying too hard. I cannot tell you how many times I have heard people say that they continued the date/relationship because it was better than nothing. This is a gargantuan fallacy and you need a serious personal evaluation before you proceed. Your personal growth is not nothing. Time spent alone, catching up with an old friend, developing a new skill, or even catching up on sleep, is more important than spending time with a person who will ultimately not work out. Jumping in with both feet and having it not work out is one thing, but knowing that this person is not for you and postponing the inevitable is wasting your time, and this person's time. Your actions in this stage of dating are highly connected to the energy fields of the universe. Finding the right person is significantly less contingent on luck than people think it may be. You are constantly sending messages to the forces that unite and repel. When you continue to spend time with a person who is not right for you, you are sending a message to the universe that you are cut off from the search. A much better match will be repelled as you will be hidden under the cloak of relationship mediocrity. When you choose to spend your time focusing on personal growth, you create space for the universe to work in ways that guide you to relationship fulfillment. The muscle you need to focus on here is patience. Patience in your mind and patience in your actions. Remember that this is your timeline, not your ex's, not your parents', and not your friends'. This is your journey and it will unfold as slowly or as quickly as it needs to unfold. Do not get in the way of that undeniable force that wants to manifest in you.

You have already taken the step that will tell the world you are ready as you will ever be to meet someone new by walking into the land of vulnerability. You put on your single status for all to see online. This is a step that takes courage, strength, and fortitude. It shows that you are no longer clinging to the past, or caught up in the mess that a divorce will inevitably produce. You have shown your ability to exert non-resistance which is a skill that only few possess. You have accepted your situation as a person that is single and looking, and with that comes great opportunity. As I write this chapter I am excited that you have made it this far. You are a champion, warrior, and a fun loving catch with a penchant for travel and pic of you on your bike. Keep your head held high as you write about your interests and hobbies. This is a club you did not sign up for, but you are making the best of every stage and about to make someone else's life feel more complete and purposeful. What could be more uplifting than that! Congratulate yourself for coming this far, be meticulous with your time, and trust that when your intentions are in line with your actions, the universe will work in ways that guide you to where you need to be.

CHECK CHECK

Please don't follow my timeline. Mine was particularly fast and not necessarily recommended. I took a solid four months to grieve and at a certain point I found myself with a handle on my own sense of happiness, in a place of confidence, and wanting some adult conversation. I was way too into reading energy fields and focusing on the present moment to presume I was looking for anything other than a stiff drink and a person to share it with. I had always known myself to be a good conversationalist and why not apply that skill to meeting someone new. My plan was only to have a conversation, and if that conversation went well, to have another conversation. However, I did not come to that place of acceptance easily. It took a serious nudge from a person close to me to get me in the ring.

"Just do it, Bern," Kai said to me with an all-knowing shrug.

"Nah, what if he finds out? He already has a girlfriend, and if he finds out that I am online dating, essentially starting from zero, it would just be too embarrassing. Can't I just try to date organically? Ya know, go on a date without exposing myself so publicly like that?"

"Nope, just do it," Kai repeated. Kai had a way of knowing what's right and not veering from it.

"What if my ex's single friends see my profile online? Oh dear God, what if one of them clicks on my profile? I'm a private person, Kai. I just can't do it."

"Fuck, that Bernie!" She said while standing in her living room that embodied post-divorce mastery. In decorating, she took the liberty of making the place look as feminine as she wanted, but in a balanced way. The walls were adorned with art, both professional and amateur, to enhance her obvious obsession with framing pictures of her beautiful daughters. Her couch said "comfy," while her chandelier said "Goddess." With her framed quotes on the end tables and glitter on the walls, the energy of her home emanated adventure, style, and soulful peace.

With a glitter pen in her hand she continued, "This is the stage you are in and there's nothing wrong with it. First of all, who the fuck cares what he sees. He is not a part of your life anymore, and you don't need to concern yourself with his thoughts on your personal life. But more importantly, you need to own your situation. Grow a pair of ovaries little sis and let yourself be vulnerable. We are all single. This was not part of our life plan, but here we are. Do you want to be the one who cowers in a corner concerned about what everyone else will think? Or do you want to be the one who owns her shit and puts herself out there? The Bernie I know stands tall and takes life by the nipples."

I absorbed the strength of her words and replied, "Maybe I just want to be the Bernie who listens to Brene Brown's Ted Talk for the hundredth time while sipping delicious coffee on her sister's couch? Can't I just be that, Bernie? That Bernie is cozy and comfortable and finding a new way to not miss her children on their weekend with their father by indulging in a slight podcast addiction."

"Are you kidding me?" she said shocked, while putting down her glitter pen and picking up her laptop. "Really? The Brene Brown Ted Talk on vulnerability? The irony isn't lost on me, sweet sister. I literally have her quotes on my end table. Here's one where she says, 'Vulnerability is not winning or losing; it's having the courage to show up and be seen when we have no control over the outcome."

"Oh yeah," she said laughing as she hopped over her red suede couch to the Brene Brown quote on her other end table. "Here she says, 'People who wade into discomfort and vulnerability and tell the truth about their stories are the real badasses.' I put that shit in frames because it's language I can sink my teeth into."

We paused and took a moment to drink up our Brene quotes like a tall glass of water.

"Wait," she carried on, "remind me what you do for a living. Bernie, this is your journey. Not his, not your small town where everyone knows each other, and not the people who you think will judge you. I'm telling you, it feels so good to just own where you are and not give a flying fuck what anyone thinks about it. Plus, putting yourself out there is a sign of strength. You are an amazing person with so much love to give! Plus, I am already halfway through setting up your profile."

"What!?" I grabbed her laptop. "That's what you've been doing?"

Every step of this process made me feel so rusty. The very idea of dating was a concept so lost on me. What were people saying on profiles these days? Which way am I supposed to swipe again? Why can't I find one picture of me without my husband in it? And why for the love of God am I still calling him my husband?

Turns out all of those questions had rather simple answers. Hi. Left for no, right for yes, I could easily cut him out, and old habits die hard. Online dating is surprisingly like going to the gym. The hardest part is getting there, and once you're done you're so glad you did it!

With her laptop in my hands I took the reins of my profile destiny. I was glad that she started it but I wanted my personality to come through. I found some pics, added a line or two about my interests, and within minutes it was live. I couldn't believe how fast it happened.

I started looking through a few profiles. "Kai, it jumped at me!" I said as I threw my phone on the couch.

"That's good! It means someone has already swiped right on your profile. The good part about this app is that you have to be the first one to start the conversation."

I started responding to matches. This part was fun. Even though I still felt as unsteady as a newborn colt, it felt good to know I was moving in a direction of onward. I had already been on a few non-dates at this point, but this was more empowering. I did not have to rely on another person to set me up with someone, or hope for some cheesy meet cute on the street. I realized that the entire process was up to me. I could go on one date per week or five. I could join one dating app or many. I could be as aggressive with the process as I wanted to be and I could not believe how satisfying that felt.

After texting one particular person for a few funny and enticing exchanges, I gave him my number and texted, "I have to hop in my car, want to chat?"

"Oh no... you didn't!" Kai said with shock on her face. "Bern, no one chats anymore. It's all through text and then you meet up somewhere. Did you really just ask him to talk on the phone? In today's dating climate, sleeping with someone is less intimate than asking them to talk on the phone! That was so aggressive. Godspeed, sweet sis."

"Listen," I said, "I'm a busy person and my thumbs are tired. Driving and chatting are an efficient use of time and I have a solid half hour before I get home. So yes, I may be acting like an online dating dinosaur, but if I'm going to do this I will have to make the process my own. Besides, the cool kids still talk on the phone, right?"

I said goodbye to her and thanked her for the nudge. I left her beautifully-balanced home and hopped into my car. I felt something in my gut already and I liked it. On the road onward, it doesn't matter how fast you go, forward is forward. For me, it took a person who knew the right path, and could lay out the steps in a language that I could understand. Kai's dialect of no bullshit resonated in a profound and lasting way.

Two minutes later I was driving home and the phone rang. "Did you really just ask me to talk on the phone? No one does that anymore," said a man's voice through the SUV phone speaker.

I spoke with a man named Jesse for my entire 30 minute ride home. He made me laugh many times which was the ultimate aphrodisiac. Equally as important, he seemed to be laughing at my quirky weird jokes, which made it more than just jokes; it was banter. We were dancing on the edge of not knowing if this person was crazy or really funny, and I liked it. I knew I definitely wanted to meet up with this guy!

I must have been doing something right because many intriguing matches were made through the dating app. The mere fact that these matches were made online put me solidly in a full ten degrees from Netflix, but even that was becoming more palatable because I was owning my situation. I enjoyed the back and forth texts with complete strangers made from my own home. I enjoyed the thrill of the hunt in a sea of possibilities. I was well aware that this enjoyment could peter out and become tedious once the newness of it wore out, but I was willing to take that risk. I knew that I was in a place of enjoyment and if that enjoyment turned tedious, I would put myself solidly in a place of acceptance.

For my particular circumstance, I decided to add layers to the concept of acceptance. I was in a state of acceptance for my situation. Divorce had arrived and it was not going anywhere. But it was because of that acceptance that I could be in a place of enjoyment regarding online dating. What could have been misconstrued as onerous became fun. When a person didn't text me back, I literally considered it his loss and moved on. It felt like a game of table tennis, and when the ball wasn't hit back, I moved on to the next player in the tournament. There was no better time to not take myself, or anyone else, too seriously. I was committed to noticing the ups and downs as part of the overall experience.

That is said with complete understanding that this endeavor can lose its luster. As the wonderful Charlotte says on Sex and the City, "I've been dating for 15 years, I'm exhausted, where is he?" This is the point where that enjoyment turns to stamina. Where table tennis turns to table clean up. This stage, if you are not in it already, is perfectly fine, too. There are so many ways to grow and develop from finding a partner right away, or not finding one. The journey is about discovering yourself, and facing the mirror in front of you in the form of a first date or a fortieth date, and is a cathartic move toward self-acceptance.

A line I use often with my patients is "action trumps anxiety." This rings true in so many ways. Quite often what our minds need is the opportunity to stop thinking and to just simply begin. Stop thinking about your move out of your home and just begin packing a box. Stop thinking about your paperwork and just begin with one file. Stop thinking about how you are going to start dating again after ten years of marriage and just go on a date. Life is so much more lively when lived outside of your head.

The Theory of Check Check

I had already spoken to Jason on the phone and he seemed easy to talk to. We had plans to meet up on Tuesday, which is why I was surprised to get a text from him on Monday asking me if I was free because he was in the area. I immediately did a personal body scan. I was in fact free. It was a beautiful 70 degree afternoon a few hours before sunset. I had the ocean in my line of sight which always brings with it a sense of calm. I was walking the boards (to all people not from New Jersey, that means walking along the beach on the boardwalk for either exercise, enjoyment, an ice cream, or a combination of those three), and knew I had at least an hour before I needed to meet up with my kids. I had some, but little makeup on, ripped jeans, my favorite Surfrider sweatshirt, and flip flops. Definitely not my usual first date attire but coincidentally a look that couldn't possibly be more me. I agreed to meet him in ten minutes at a boardwalk bench that I knew would take me ten minutes to walk to.

Perfect. Anxiety: low. Time for preparation and overthinking every detail: non-existent. Degrees from Netflix: a mere 2. The low degree was because I had already spoken to him and knew he could carry on a conversation with ease; we were meeting in a public place, and I really did not have to go out of my way at all. It felt like bumping into someone during a leisurely walk. Since anxiety comes from thoughts about moments other than the one you are in, I liked what little time I had to prepare for this date.

I walked at a flip flop pace to a side of the boardwalk where I knew that my chances of running into someone I knew significantly dropped. And again for the people not from this area of the Jersey Shore, this is a thing as well. There is a very strong and loyal sense of localism when it comes to beach choice. You buy your beach badge for a particular section of beach which usually consists of a one mile stretch. Each section is known for very different aspects depending on the town it represents. Some sections are known to be family oriented, some are known for parties, etc. You choose your section based upon your needs, and that becomes your beach. Year after year, the same people come to the same portion of their stretch of boardwalk and adjoining beach. This holds true even more so when you live in a beach town that is connected to said boardwalk. This is where localism multiplies tenfold, because by living in the town you have basically double downed on your love for the area. Crossing over to another town becomes unheard of. You ride your beach cruiser bicycle to your section and eat up every part of it.

That was why, with some level of confidence, I knew I could walk ten minutes north and feel a sense of anonymity.

After all, it is one thing to decide to begin a journey of online dating, and another to run into acquaintances while doing it. I walked over the line that divides one town from another, and right into my first post-divorce on-purpose date.

He sat right on the bench that we discussed, donning his casual style and smokey blues. He stood up to greet me and went right in for the hug. *Oh, is that how dates start? Ok,* I thought.

We exchanged pleasantries and had a great conversation while watching dolphins swim by in the ocean. I felt calm and confident the whole way through. He asked questions and my answers were charming and funny, although not quite mem-orable enough to recount. He was nice and interesting enough, and by the end of the date I couldn't help thinking, *Wow, this guy is such a great catch. I wonder if there is any-one I can set him up with?* I know this doesn't make sense, but it was my truth. He had all the boxes checked in terms of mate finding. I appreciated his witty banter and more im-portantly his honesty. He was just a few years older than I was and did not have children. In my biggest moment of both courage and intrigued, I asked him the question that was plaguing me the most.

"You are really ok with the fact that I have two humans that follow me around everywhere?"

His response revealed the most appreciated piece of honesty I had ever heard from someone on a first date. "I don't like to date women who are too much younger than I am, and I know women in our age category generally have children. It's really just something I've accepted and don't mind at all. I just consider it part of the overall package."

I felt like hugging him again. It was just so honest, and it was also the moment that I made yet another very personal choice. It was not a forever decision, but it was a decision I knew would serve me for the stage that I was in. I only wanted to date men who also had children. I say this with as much reserve and respect as a person possibly can. There are so many amazing, childless catches out there, and I didn't want to discount them. But if I were living my truth, I had to keep my "to be understood is divine" blah blah as my high priority.

I felt like he would not be able to understand me. I had dedicated just about all of my adult life to the pursuit of having and raising children. They were, are, and always will be the loves of my life. Just that morning I suffered a minor elbow injury because my children and I were trying to make a human pyramid. They both toppled over me in a fit of laughter. Their giggles came from a place that was so genuine and sweet that it left me out of breath and in awe. I was unable to use my right arm for hours after, but I would not have changed that moment for the world. Kids have a way of beating you down in the most delicious and unexplainable ways. I just couldn't fathom entering into a relationship with someone who didn't fully understand that.

When he texted me the next day to ask if he could take me out to dinner on our actual planned date night, I respectfully declined. A better match was out there waiting for me and I didn't want to miss it.

This, of course, was arguable. A compassionate person can find ways to understand a life story different than his. There was also a certain amount of convenience in dating someone who doesn't have children just in terms of free time and flexibility. But for this aspect, just this one seemingly all-encompassing aspect, I decided to honor what I felt. And what I wanted was to narrow my search for only men who already had children.

Has children: doesn't want more. Check check.

Water seeks its own level. I had children and didn't want more. That was what I wanted to find in the person with whom I was looking to have a conversation. I knew that if the conversation were to lead to another conversation, it would at some point lead to my insatiable love for my kids. It was a love that was just too important not to share in an experiential way.

However, this admonition led me to the end of the internet. Or, at least, the internet according to my dating app. I swiped left so many times that I got left thumb fatigue. A syndrome just left of carpal tunnel. When you reach the end of the internet, the app asks you to change your filters so that it can show you more matches. What!? Change my standards so that I could have more chances at false starts? No thank you.

Clearly what I needed was a break from dating. My personal philosophy had always been to focus on the next right step. Going on one date felt right, and taking a break from it also felt right. I wanted the slow approach to dating and that included a substantial hiatus from the entire scene. I went on one date and felt very accomplished, and empowered. I had put myself out there in the post-divorce dating world which took the aforementioned courage, fortitude, and strength. After all of that, I was a bit exhausted from the whole thing. This was an integral part of my maintenance of balance. I wanted to refocus from that feeling of searching to the feeling of gratitude for what I already had.

I decided to angle my attention on all the love that was already surrounding me. With the first date hurdle behind me, I could once again pour myself into my spiritual journey and my friends that had known me for a lifetime. I dialed in to the sweet, simple pleasures of being romantically unattached.

One weekend, since I was a party of one, I called up my friend Skylar who was the only person I knew to be just as spontaneous as I was. "Hey, you don't have plans tomorrow do you?" I asked.

"No, of course not. That's a full 24 hours away and you know that is way too future thinking for me." Skylar had this combination reply to everything. She was extremely direct from years of being an attorney, but also refreshingly laid back from years of owning her personality.

"Great, I just booked us an overnight stay at a creepy nature spa. You in?"

"I'm packing my bags right now."

The spa was luxurious but also rugged. It was like they wanted their guests to connect to their granola routes just as much as pampered indulgences. Upon arrival, I walked in to see Skylar at the main cafeteria already in a robe and slippers, drinking coffee, and looking like an ad for 'Relaxation Weekly.' Seeing her felt like I was instantly transported from my suburban town to a pure escape. After a full morning of massage, she and I decided to relax in the lanai and watch our worries float away. The serenity of the indoor/outdoor space caused our conversation to be about nothing other than the word itself. We contemplated the word lanai from all angles. Where did it come from? Who uses that word? Had we been in a lanai before and not known it?

Hours into our mini vaca, we decided to put on our hiking boots to discover the more rugged side of the resort. We took our very relaxed brains and hit the trails. We quickly discovered that we were both solidly not foragers of the wooded terrain. We got so lost while hiking, and midway through discovered that neither of us brought water. Although it was a perfect spring day, and the forest was beautiful, we were thirsty, tired, and drained. The natural next step would have been to find a map on our phones, but we could not stop laughing for long enough to do that. Instead, we decided to Facetime our two friends so that they could be a part of the hilarity. We knew we were making a great story while we were making it and needed witnesses. Both Ellie and Rachel sat on the phone for a solid five minutes marveling at our lack of plan.

"You didn't bring a map?" Rachel said in astonishment.

"They didn't bring water! That is the most essential component of any workout. Why on earth would they think to bring a map?" Ellie chimed in before we had a chance to reply.

"But guys, look at this view!" Skylar said as she flipped her phone to show them a panoramic view of the Shawangunk Mountains.

"Ok, I have to admit I'm a little jealous. That looks absolutely beautiful. But you know if Rachel or I were there, you would have had a backpack full of supplies and a map!"

That was true. They were the planners. But Skylar and I were the ones who were free on a moment's notice. It was that connection to freedom that kept us laughing all the way back to the starting point dehydrated, exhausted, happy, and thankful for it all. That taste of freedom also helped me to channel my sense of independence. I didn't have to check in with anyone, or ask if the expenditure was appropriate, or worry that my absence was disappointing anyone. It was my weekend off from the kids and those were the freedoms of single life. I decided to relish in them for as long as they were mine. That weekend we made memories that I'm not sure would have happened if I had been consumed by a hunt for something else.

In Trouble

Just as empowering as it was to set the pace of my dating life, it was equally as empowering to enjoy solitude. I had been calling an array of friends and setting up fun adventures with each of them. I was on a 'friend high.' I thought of the possibility that they could possibly be all I needed. On one weekend I had my girls (little), and the next weekend I had my girls (big). Even though I historically preferred to be in a relationship, I set that feeling aside for a while and felt fulfilled. My personal balance meter was in check. The harmony continued, until my phone surprisingly buzzed.

It wasn't my dating app as I had not checked it for weeks. It was that guy Jesse. The initial funny one who made me laugh for 30 minutes straight, and then after a few interesting text exchanges, faded. Did he fade because I asked him to talk on the phone instead of text, thereby showing my dinosaur approach to online dating? Was it because I told him that I had majority custody of my two children? The latter was a point that I did not consider a mistake, but that sis Kai told me may have scared him off.

"New Jersey is generally a 50/50 state," she said. "Telling a guy that you have majority custody within the first convo might seem like a tough nut to swallow."

The point was that I didn't care. Before actually meeting up with a person in the online dating scene, it was almost always about timing. Your profile could be absolutely perfect, but if the timing wasn't right, it was a no-go. The timing for me worked out; plus, if this guy could make me laugh that much on the phone, I just had to see if he could do it again in person. It was sheer curiosity that got me to risk my friend high to see just what this guy had to offer.

"Yes," I said. "Friday night sounds great."

But fuck, Friday night was two nights away which gave me way too much time to stew in anticipatory anxiety. I thought it was important that he drive to my town because I'm old school, but that unearthed another slew of problems. My turf meant being at a bar where I could possibly be spotted by someone I knew. Friday night plans also meant I needed to hire a sitter and kiss my children goodbye for the night knowing that I was going to meet a total stranger. There were a lot of firsts happening, and each one needed to be calculated on a risk management chart.

"Breath, Bern," the inner dialogue began. "This is just going to be a conversation, at a bar, with a man who has never been your husband."

So there it was. Even the woman who dedicated her career to helping people work through their anxiety, experienced anxiety. Even the person who had the most intense of spiritual awakenings could have trouble staying present minded. As my mom put it, "the weeds just grow." As grounded and centered as you may be one day, the next can trigger events that bring you to a place of emotional upheaval.

I opened up my guru study guide and did my best to stay in the moment. As I got ready for my date and felt my hands clam up in that sweaty, nervous way, I thought back to my training in mindfulness practices. Sometimes, especially during times of total nervousness, the trick is not to wish the nervousness away, but just to be aware of it.

Mindfulness is defined by Wikipedia as "a mental state achieved by focusing one's awareness on the present moment, while calmly acknowledging and accepting one's feelings, thoughts, and bodily sensations, used as a therapeutic technique." It is also defined as the self-regulation of attention with an attitude of curiosity, openness, and acceptance.

I looked down at my sweaty hands and reminded myself that this was my strength. Because of my profession and years of therapy, I was quite well versed at working through difficult emotions. Dating post-divorce is hard, but I was doing it anyway. It was even more difficult because I was truly interested in him. The curiosity component of mindfulness made it just a tad easier. I was so curious about the evening that I could use it as a way to further my spiritual journey. I welcomed the challenge because I was able to experience it from the standpoint of both an observer of the situation, and the one going through it. The observer knew it was all going to work out ok because stretching yourself furthers personal growth regardless of outcomes. The one going through it felt nervous and excited and was trying to minimize expectations. I kept my awareness of both of those attributes and put one foot in front of the other.

I took one last look in the mirror, kissed my kids goodbye, and sat on the porch. I observed myself feeling excited, and then I observed the flood of emotion. It was a scene that had played out so many times before. In my old life, my husband would text me to let me know that he was outside waiting in the car, usually on the phone with a client, and ready for date night. It wasn't thoughts of him that were tripping me up, but rather the habitual cadence that a night out used to take. I would kiss the kids, talk to the sitter, and then hop into his car. There was no nervousness to that scenario. Hopping into his car was guaranteed fun. There was an inherent and obvious knowing of a person. Safe. Comfortable. Exciting. The decadently delicious food provided the last touch on a winner of a combination. Back in the days of marriage, date nights were our strong suit. It was just the rest of life that brought us trouble. So sitting there, on the porch, after the rush of date night happenstance and kissing the kids goodbye, I felt like maybe my brain was moving just a step faster than my legs. Was it all too fast?

And there it went again. The thoughts in my head were tripping up a perfectly wonderful moment of onward movement and spiritual curiosity. "Stop thinking, Bern, and send for an Uber." I once again took mind that action trumps anxiety and got my feet to begin working again. I felt the direction forward both physically and mentally.

As a rather punctual person, if I arrive somewhere late there is usually a purposeful reason for it. Online dating at 40 was hard enough, and I certainly didn't need to be the first one at the bar glancing up every time the door opened. Nope, that was his job. He texted me exactly where he was sitting at the bar and I arrived promptly ten minutes late.

I had already solved one sweaty hand problem in the Uber by masterfully wiping my hands on my jeans, but I was at a loss about what to do about the insane case of dry mouth. It was another symptom of my nervousness, and although I was very accepting of that part of the situation, actually I thought it rather comical, I did not know how to fix it before walking into the restaurant. I had to embrace it. Embrace and pray for water.

I scanned the room. It was crowded but not packed during that time of night when happy hour turned to dinner. The late spring sun was still pouring into the room, offering a mix of natural and overhead light. I saw Jesse and recognized him instantly. He stood up to give me a hug hello with a genuine, adorable smile on his face. His brown eyes and boyish charm came through in person just as much as it did in his pictures. I liked how he stood to greet me and showed me my seat that he reserved at the crowded bar. With the catfish scenario out of the way, the nerves dissolved into pure calm enjoyment, but dry mouth does not go away without water.

Another wonderful skill that I learned by being a therapist was the art of keeping another person talking. This skill comes in handy in the therapist chair, and apparently also during extreme bouts of dry mouth. Open ended questions were my friend.

Outer dialogue, "So how was your day?"
Inner dialogue, "Where's that fucking bartender?"
Outer dialogue, "That's so interesting, tell me more."
Inner dialogue, "For fuck's sake, why the slowness?"
Outer dialogue, "Yes, hi, water would be great!"
Inner dialogue, "For the love of God bartender, can you move any faster."

As soon as that first sip of lemony water hit my desert of a palate, it was like the conversation gods unleashed me from my tethered shackles. It was not at all lost on me though that when I really needed him to talk, he did. He told me one funny story after another keeping me laughing through my maniacal inner dialogue. Did he know I needed him to talk? Did he sense it on some level? Or was he just really good at responding to open-ended questions? It didn't matter. All I felt was lucky. Lucky that the babysitter worked out, lucky to have a night dedicated to much needed adult conversation, and present minded enough to soak in all of it at once.

He sent some questions my way, and with my water nearby, I was more than happy to answer them. One conversation was turning into another and I wasn't about to stop any of them. The flow was ridiculous and the ability to stay present became effortless.

I had learned from previous online dating experiences from when I was in my twenties to never sign up for a long time commitment. Which basically meant, commit to a coffee, a drink, or a walk on the boards, but don't commit to dinner. That was a long process and if you knew within the first five minutes that this person was not for you, the night would be long and tedious, or short and filled with hunger pangs. As a result, it became my modus operandi to commit to something short, and if it went well, we would graduate to something longer.

On this date, not only did one conversation turn into another, but I found myself magnetized to every word. "You do this thing when you laugh," he said. "You look away for a strikingly adorable moment before I get your gaze back again."

He has known me for two hours, I thought. *How can he read me with such detail already? Yes, yes, yes, we are definitely graduating to dinner.*

"You could do some serious people watching from here," he said as we arrived at our table that was overlooking the street below. The town was filled with people excited to be outside after the long winter. There was no longer the bundled brisk walk from one restaurant to another as seen only one month prior. People were now lingering on the street happy to take their time in the fresh air. I connected with the energy of it. It was like the world and I were simultaneously opening up and taking the extra time to absorb the details.

Shortly after our meal, which I devoured with the grace of a hungry linebacker, we continued to talk about everything and nothing, when the most pensive look came over his face as he said, "You are amazing... he is crazy."

This was the most loaded statement of the evening and I didn't know exactly how to take it. Thank you with a shoulder shrug? I took a breath in and lost my ability to exhale. Hearing that someone found me amazing was quite the ego boost and apropos for a first date. Especially one that was going so well. But the "he is crazy" part raised so many questions. Did he read an article on things to say to recently divorced women while on a date? Was it just an extension of the first portion of the flattering statement? He knew nothing of me, and certainly nothing of my ex. He didn't even know my last name. How could he have known that I had been grappling with that very sentiment for months? Could he smell the ashes from the dumpster fire of a life situation still lingering on my skin? Could he sense that although I was effervescently happy in the moment, I had recently come out of intense pain? Not possible. I kept that shit hidden like a dead body in the trunk. I was a master compartmentalizer who lived in the moment like Mahatma Fucking Ghandi.

But still, buried deep down lay the resounding question in my mind, "How could he leave me?" And then, while struggling to get the cherry out of my drink, Jesse answered the question with three simple words. Could it have been that simple? "He. is. crazy." Most assuredly I was crazy too, but that was not the focus of the conversation. My thoughts left the table and our date for just a moment as the inner dialogue turned to "maybe I don't have to pick apart 12 years of the relationship equivalent of an upstream swimming salmon. Maybe I don't have to blame myself for those moments when I acted human. Maybe I could just admonish his lunacy and call it a day!" The prospect was mind blowing and cathartic, but I knew I needed to bring myself back to the moment in which I was living. I thanked him for the flattering comment and suggested we order another round of tacos. This girl was hungry.

We went on to talk about our lives and situations and dove into the pool of the divorce topic without diving too deep. The elevator speech of family upheaval basically comes down to:

1. Time separated or divorced.
2. Children? How many?
3. Level of current involvement with the ex.
4. Brief understanding of the reason for the divorce.

The fourth being the most complicated part of the elevator speech because this type of situation can never be surmised in one sentence, but can give a general understanding of both your past and personal character. Some common sentences include, "we were married too young," "we were like roommates for so many years," "we didn't see eye to eye on things," etc. These sentences give a brief starting point to pick back up many dates later. They reveal so much by what they are not saying. They don't place blame and they don't accuse. Someone with the line "he was a selfish prick who did not care" would be saying that there was still a lot of work to do in terms of working through residual anger and personal refinement. The key was to give enough detail to sound genuine, while having enough reservations to keep it respectful.

I was already privy to the fact that he had two great kids and didn't want more (check check), but I didn't know the details therein. One of the most delectable parts of a first date is the process of discovery. Most people have certain facts written on their profile. "Divorced father of two seeking long term relationship." This is an informative starting point, but it does not show anything more than fact. What caught my attention, and left me unstitched, was the way Jesse spoke about his kids. He could not stop smiling as he told me bits and pieces about each one. His eyes lit up with such light, such glowing happiness, that I knew he was one of my people. And by 'my people' I mean involved parent. Parenting is one of the hardest things I have ever done, but also the most rewarding and enjoyable. An involved parent knows the challenge/blessing ratio. He showed his true passion when he said "Taking them to the beach is one of my favorite things to do on this planet" with that glow in his eyes and an undeniable smile coming through his beard. You just can't capture that shit in a profile!

When a first date feels like an interview, there is a high likelihood that it will not be followed by a second. Even if every question is answered exquisitely and articulately, it will still feel like work. With our precious few moments that we adults have after the grind of adulting, we really don't want our Friday nights to feel like work. This particular date did not feel like work. It felt like magic. Therapists are, fortunately or unfortunately, very attuned to the cadence of a conversation. We are aware when a conversation begins to feel like a session, which is when people talk about themselves entirely too much. Or on the flip side when it begins to feel like an archeological dig, which is when we are pulling and reaching to get the other person to talk at all. But when two people are in flow, the therapist hat goes out the window. All that is left is you, and him, and a world to explore.

That was certainly the case on this particular date. Hours after the date began, he drove his Jeep Wrangler up to my driveway to drop me off. "You're fun!" I said to him. I felt like his personality was like a custom built playground made specifically for me.

"I had such an amazing time with you! When can I see you again?" Like a true salesman, he knew how to keep the relationship going. We set the time of our next date and I walked back into my life. I was still smiling as I walked back onto the porch that had witnessed the scene of so much anxiety only hours earlier. I knew a milestone had been crossed and I would never go back to the other side of it again.

I got home that night at one o'clock in the morning! That was extremely late considering I only signed up to meet for one drink.

"Guys, I have to tell you about the past six hours!" I said to my video messaging app that Ellie, Rachel, Skylar and I had been using for years. And yes, can someone give a shout out to middle schoolers everywhere? There are some things that just don't change. The need to divulge every detail of a date with your girlfriends begins in middle school and apparently just doesn't end. The only difference between now and then is that technology has become infinitely better and we don't have curfews.

Gone are the days of beeping your friends (fyi to the younger generations, beepers were a thing, look them up), and then going on 777-films so that when they called back, it would be received as call waiting instead of a call to the house that would otherwise wake the entire house up. As your other friends "beeped in," you could include everyone on the chat and your parents would be none the wiser. Needless to say, life has gotten so much better since middle school.

Instead, my silent late night video message went directly to Ellie, Rachel, and Skylar. The real time details of that date were captured as my seventh-grade persona came leaping out of me in the form of juicy gossip.

"We had so much fun."

"It was a full 10 degrees from Netflix."

"I am so glad I went. He's just so fun, and cute, and funny! Shit you guys, I am in trouble with this one."

When a woman says "I'm in trouble with this one," it is actually a good thing. It means that she can no longer live in a state of nonchalance. There is something comforting about truly not caring whether or not he calls. Ambivalence means you have the upper hand, because you truly don't care if you see this person again. But if you like someone, or as my daughter says, "like'm like'm," then it is admitting that it would be a let down if this person doesn't feel the same way.

I gave my friends the details I needed to divulge, then put my phone away feeling that sense of download that happens after a great conversation, even though the conversation was essentially with myself. Post trauma or heartbreak it is common for people to say "Call me anytime! Even if it's the middle of the night I'm here for you." But we all know that you never will. Those middle of the night moments need to happen on your own, in your own terms, and with your own coping mechanisms.

Before falling asleep, I needed to recenter. Stay balanced. Stay in the moment. One good date did not mean it was going to turn into an actual relationship, but it did mean that I, at 40 years old and dating in the post-divorce world, could have one good date. I could go out, meet someone new, and have a fantastic time while doing it. I felt myself emerging on my own.

At that moment, that was all I needed to feel.

Moving On In Summation

- Get back out there in whatever way feels natural to you.

- Know yourself and what you are looking for in terms of a date or any other new chapter activity.

- Vulnerability and courage are one in the same. Own that shit!

CHAPTER SIX

DROP YOUR EGO

The PDR

The Post Divorce Relationship (PDR) is significantly more complex than pre-divorce. In the pre-divorce world, the progression is more linear. You fall in love and then combine your worlds. In the PDR, both worlds have exponentially grown, making them significantly more difficult to combine. The picture involves kids, more substantial careers, and more ties to the life that had been in place. Both people have developed roots that have grown into their lives, making it harder to uproot and join with another person.

I was not aware of the logistical difficulties of the PDR until I rubbed up against them, and it didn't take very long for that to happen. Jesse and I were on our third date fully still in the stage of getting to know each other. We sat on a bench overlooking the Navesink River after a leisurely hike through the woods (Jesse brought water, gluten free granola bars, extra sweatshirts, and didn't need a map). It was the perfect place to enjoy the view and catch our breath after the hike. The sun was still high in the sky and the boats in the Navesink were starting their season in the spring air. I was enjoying my time with him immensely and didn't want to cut it short, but my kids were due to come back from being with their father. The next step was back to his Wrangler and then back to my world.

"So when can I get more of that Bernie time?" Jesse said in a way that seemed both hungry and satiated.

"I don't know," I said. "We are both on separate weekends." Which, in the divorce world, means that our weekends were not in sync in terms of kid detail. "How is that going to work?"

His answer was so succinct and perfect. "We'll figure it out."

I was so good at the date part of our interaction... the talking, the laughing, and the flirting. Conversation was my jam, especially with him. But figuring out the part about dating in the post-divorce world, with two sets of kids, and two different schedules registered as stupefying. It was too early in the relationship for one of us to switch weekends for the other, plus we were at completely different points of the divorce process. He was completely done and settled into his new life of separate homes and joint custody. I was still in the place that exists when the separation was concrete but the actual divorce/life was not finalized.

So how were we supposed to start a relationship while I was still stuck in legally separated limbo? "We'll figure it out." When were we supposed to sync up our weekends? "We'll figure it out." When were we supposed to let people know, let our kids know, introduce our kids, blend our lives, families and worlds? "We'll figure it out." One step at a time, one conversation at a time, we figured it all out. And later, when I would get ahead of myself with questions or adjustments because I felt we were moving too fast, or too slow, or too perfect, he knew just how to make the world stop so that we could glide through the next right step.

"We'll figure it out." That was everything I had been studying for months wrapped up into one little sentence. With one shrug it was like he was saying... "I don't know, Beautiful, but we have right now so let's live it up. When the next situation presents itself, we will know exactly what to do because that is the situation we will be in at the time, and even though this is only our third date, this is already us."

The best part about being in a relationship is that there are (usually) two people in it. There are more complications, but there are also two people with equal skin in the game rising to make it work. As the months went by, Rachel's advice from just a few months prior, "If you put even a fraction of the amount of effort into your next relationship as you did with this dysfunctional one, you will be shocked at the return," certainly came to fruition. I was in awe at how putting effort into the relationship didn't seem like effort at all. The effort was reciprocated in that synergistic way whereas my one, plus his one, equaled five.

My time spent with him encompassed all the joys and surprises inherent in learning someone new. My time spent without him continued to be entangled with separating myself from my ex both circumstantially and emotionally. Jesse could see what I was presenting on the surface as well as the undercurrent of grief that I continued to work through. I was still learning to handle life as a solo operation. I knew that I could no longer rely on my ex as a partner in crime, but those skills of independence needed to be relearned. Coming upon my own ground was less about my ex than it was about letting go of the dream of the future that once seemed so clear. The heart is a very complex worrier. It can fall in love while simultaneously grieving a life long gone. Readjusting my life from the interdependence of the marital state to independence and solo-parenting of the post marital state took time and effort.

Side note: solo parenting is very different from single parenting. Single parents truly have all the responsibilities fall directly on them. While solo parents have another person, or co-parent, to share in the responsibilities; but it is separated, so that when you are on, you are on. Your time with your children is all you. There is no co-conspirator, no divide and conquer, and no tagging out. When you are off, when the kids are with their other parent, you are totally off. It is intense and extremely different from married life.

For example, my ex used to fix the toys. I would clean them, he would fix them. Now I do both. My dad gave me a toolbox full of tools upon moving into my first apartment. It collected dust while I was married. Post-separation it turned into one of my most prized possessions. Turning into Bob the Builder was not the hard part. Change and adjusting to that change was the hard part, and it took time to recalibrate.

My relationship with Jesse flourished while all of this was going on. He had been through the rigors of divorce and was aware of the precariousness of the process. Some weeks were more stressful than others and as much as I tried to hide it, he could see it written all over my face. He could read that I needed a slow pace. He could see when my stress levels called for a night of levity, and would plan out a fun activity to match that pace.

When feelings and emotions began to intensify, he continued to modify his pace to adapt to my seemingly stressful world. Instead of coming right out with "I love you," he would say, "I have very strong feelings for you but I don't want to say it because I don't want to freak you out." I wanted him to say it, but his awareness of my needs meant so much more than the words. I was floored by how perceptive and understanding a person could be. Also, he was totally on point. I needed a slow pace, and anything faster would have freaked me out.

I felt like I was seen, heard, and understood. He was getting the stronger me. The person who had the confidence to know that I would continue to get stronger every day. Then when I was totally ready and comfortable in the place that the relationship had taken us, I was ready for the words we had both been thinking for months. "We're in love, aren't we?" I said.

He replied with, "We have been for a long time."

He got the stronger me because he knew she was within me and waited for her to come out. I got the stronger him because he had been through his own storm and was fully ready for his next chapter. Divorce was hard, but this level of personal actualization was another silver lining.

When stress came our way, he said, "You got me shook (his word), I'm in this regardless of what gets thrown our way. It would take a lot more than (insert bullshit here) to get me away." Stress needs to happen in a relationship to show you what you've got. But especially in the PDR, you need to see if your ways of handling that stress are in line. You are both coming to the relationship as an older, wiser person. There is less uninformed optimism and more realism. The older, wiser you is going to put up with less and expect more. But that goes both ways. The person you are dating won't put up with your shit and also wants to see your more evolved self.

No pressure, but bring your A game. The key here is knowing that your A game includes your stronger, more vulnerable self. It's about bringing both your dark sides and your light. It's putting up a front that you are totally ok, and absorbing his words as he says, "You're not, but you will tell me when you're ready." Then 20 minutes later letting it all come out as he dries your tears on his shirtsleeve. The PDR is not always pretty. It is inherently more complex with extremely far reaching differences. The differences include children of all ages or not all, exes who are still in the picture to varying degrees, and lives coming apart at the seams to be put back together with a completely new stitch. You are not beginning your adult life with another person but rather recreating it from the middle. There are no standards for how it's done because no one planned to be there.

The reason why I said that there is no sure way to know if you are ready to begin a new relationship is because it has little to do with linear time. It has more to do with that insane ego of yours and how far you have dropped it. It is when you have acknowledged your inner child, comforted her and healed her. When you are ready to say, "This is me, bare and broken. I can't be judged for the things that I have because they are not really mine, or the things I don't have because

I'm not attached to them anyway. This is me past the fire but still breathing in the smoke." It's when you have dropped your attachments to all that you thought made you the person that you were, and realized that your true egoless self had been waiting within you all along. It took something big, big like a cataclysmic mother fucker of a divorce, to drop the unneeded shell and emerge as the warrior that you are. When this person rises, you are ready for the next big thing. That next big thing can emerge in the form of a relationship, a volunteer effort, a creative endeavor, or even just the ability to truly enjoy a backyard bbq. Wherever you are in your journey, your next step is arriving little by little as you drop the ego that prevented you from seeing your journey at all.

You are not your perceived identity. But don't identify with that, because that will just be creating a whole new identity based on not having an identity. The ego is a difficult one to explain. Dropping my ego helped me to prioritize some of the noise that kept me up at night, and then turned it off. It was clunky and awkward at first as I had to keep reminding myself.

"I am not my roles. I am not my emotions. I am not my thoughts. I am the silent observer." I had to keep reminding myself of this distance between thought/emotions, and being, because at first it didn't come naturally. I had to keep working at being bare.

From this came the ability to let life unfold less burdened by needless worry. I did not bring expectations for how I thought life should be because I didn't have any. I let go of maintaining my value of having a nuclear family because I was no longer burdened by concepts thought up by people before me. The idea of the nuclear family was painted with a very broad stroke and doesn't work for everyone. Holding on to a thought structure that wasn't working for me or my family was causing me pain. I could not have experienced the truth of that until stripping the parts of me that were clinging to that ideal. Once I felt my true self emerge weightless and without judgment, I never wanted to pick up the weight of expectations again. I had experienced the bareness of being stripped of all that I knew to be important, and remained obstinate in holding true to that state of being. I was my breath and my next right step, always.

As a result, I enjoyed spending my time with a person who naturally lived by the same philosophy. When it came to starting a relationship, Jesse and I didn't go from dating to being committed in one definitive action. The couple that we are now existed during that first date, and I'm pretty sure we both knew it. We both came into it bare, raw, and without expectations. We let the unity reveal itself as it wanted to be revealed. It's the same for right now because the story is still unfolding one conversation at a time.

Generally, expectations are hot and heavy at the first blush of marriage. They are surrounded with pomp and circumstance that can be alarming and addicting. There's this boundless promise of hopes and dreams. There are visions of picket fences, future children, and well wishes for a bright and happy future. At the first breath of engagement there is a list of long awaited events. There is a dress to buy, a hall to book, and flowers to pick out. There is the excitement of combining two families, two lives, and so many future dreams. It is very difficult not to get disappointed given this level of grandeur. In a perfect world, the soaring expectations of a first marriage would be mitigated by a sense of grounding from the start. But until that happens, it will have to be relegated to relationships that take place post-divorce.

Sometimes Jesse and I would laugh at the amount of pressure inherent in a marriage and vow never to put that type of pressure on each other. He has had a deep understanding of what didn't work for him the first time around and so do I. He has done his own relationship autopsy and it shows because of his understanding of himself and his ability to articulate it. I could hear this ability in his voice when he said, "My friends are coming over today to watch a football game, you have a million things going on in your world with your kids, so feel free to come by but no pressure." This sounds small but it translates as huge. There was no expectation that I was *supposed* to show love by contorting into what a relationship was *supposed* to look like. Since life's proverbial pieces were up in the air, we could let them fall in a way that worked for only us, the only two people who were actually in the relationship.

The PDR, and this includes all levels of status from "just talking" to fully married, do not have to be intertwined with soaring expectations. They exist because they exist, not because they are meant to produce something beyond the relationship itself. For the second go around, this person owes you nothing in terms of fulfilling your dreams. You are arriving at the gate as a more whole person and you don't need those dreams fulfilled by another. It leaves space for just the relationship to exist and be its own entity. Relationship sans frontiers. Since there are no expectations to fill, you are liberated from the weight of them.

THE INTERVENTION FALLACY

The weeds just grow. I have seen the cycle in my office so many times. Someone starts a therapeutic intervention, be it meditation, behavior modification, medication etc., and it works. It works so well, in fact, that over time the person begins to wonder if the intervention is needed at all anymore. The intervention subsides and the person believes that he or she can coast onward without it. The coasting works swimmingly for a period of time, until it doesn't.

It is during these times that the weeds begin to grow. The thoughts, the insecurities, and the pressure begins to mount. Like accumulating snow on the ground that builds overnight, the person wakes up to an avalanche of emotion. All it takes is one trigger to set off issues that were previously thought left behind. Since the intervention is no longer in place, these issues become hard to handle at best, and extremely life disrupting at worst.

In its most simplistic form, keeping the interventions in place is the antidote. If you know that it's working, then just keep on keeping on so that you can prevent the inevitable backslide. But, when dealing with matters of human emotions, we are all susceptible to the evolution of human behaviors, and the urge to return to "normalcy." What we often forget is that using the tools that help us navigate our lives are a part of our new normal. For whatever reason, our old normal was not working for us, hence the need to make changes that are lasting. Fooling ourselves into thinking that we can have all the benefits that existed while utilizing these tools, can still exist without them. This fallacy is a part of the growth pattern. Some of us only need to learn this lesson once, while some of us need to learn this lesson many times until the pattern is brought to awareness.

It is the job of a therapist to recognize when a patient is falling prey to the intervention fallacy. In fact, we wait for it. We have seen it play out so many times that we can see the pattern unfold. We see the intervention as it's implemented, followed by the coasting, and then by the fallacy that the intervention is no longer needed. This is the point that many people stop going to therapy because they think that it is no longer needed. For many people, the actual act of going to therapy *is* the intervention. As therapists, if we see a person reverting to old behavior, we can only do so much. Aside from emotional hazard cones, we can only help the person to bring the awareness to the pattern so that they see it for themselves. Hopefully they will see that this is all a part of the process, and that the ebb and flow will continuously exist as the understanding of homeostasis continues to shift. There is nothing wrong with making changes to "what works," as long as those changes are made with awareness. For example, if a person feels that they no longer have time for their morning meditation, and instead incorporates it into their walk to work, then this is done with full knowledge and awareness. That is an example of moving with life as daily needs change and accounting for them. If, however, the daily meditation falls by the wayside without notice, well, that's when the weeds just grow.

The Intervention Fallacy is one that I like working with because it is part of a growth pattern. But like so many other human propensities, it is easier to recognize in other people than it is in myself. And, alas, the Intervention Fallacy came creeping into my world without warning and certainly without invitation.

The coast was great! I found myself in a place where I could wake up and immediately get on with my day without having to slow the forward movement of a busy day. Why take ten minutes every morning to meditate when I could just use that time to get a head start on my day? Why spend that time working on myself, I thought, if the self that I was displaying was pretty darn good! Apparently, I thought I could have all the benefits of a well-balanced person without doing any of the work that made me, well, balanced. Until...

"Hey Bern, look at this!" Kai said with concern in her eyes. "Your man has an active online dating account."

"Ha ha, he looks adorable," I said in response. "But wait, is that a new photo?"

I happen to be extremely adept at dissecting the fuck out of photos. I have done this for work, for fun, and for helping friends and family see things they cannot see while browsing through dating sites. I can spot a catfisher from a mile away. I can spot a disingenuous smile like a detective with laser vision. It actually gives me pleasure to extrapolate themes from groupings of photos. For example, when six out of the seven pics on a profile are of a man at the gym, it is important to note. When all five pics of a profile show a person holding a stiff drink, it is important to note for an entirely different reason. It is not any single one of these photos that is the issue, but the theme that they are portraying. If I could list this skill as one of my hobbies, I certainly would, but there is just no way to say "fine tooth combing profile pics" as a hobby and not sounding like a complete stalker.

But here, as luck would have it, I had the opportunity to fine tooth comb a pic on the profile of the man I was madly in love with and had been dating for seven months. "Active profile, you say? Let's just look a bit closer."

From that moment and on to the next hour, it was like I invited the most potent of triggers to head for my heart with explosive speed. The thoughts in my head were malicious and surprisingly convincing. "You never really know anyone, do you?" "Someone could have a whole other life and you would be none the wiser." "Don't be stupid," and on and on.

We all want to think that we learn from past experiences. We want to think that if we were caught off guard once, that we would be certain to not let it happen again. I had never been in a situation like this before and was not calling from direct personal experience. I was calling from an intense inner place of fear, and in seeing a completely innocuous, old profile, I thought that I needed to become a detective to safeguard myself from getting the rug pulled from under me. What could have been a joke between my boyfriend and I about how funny it is that old profiles surface at weird times turned into an accusatory missile attack straight from my wounded heart. Like an injured animal, I recoiled and then snapped at any attempt at logic.

As it was happening, I had no idea I was acting from this place of fear. My logical brain was literally atrophying with every new emotion that was felt. My thoughts were influencing my emotions, and my emotions were influencing my thoughts. It left me spinning in a web of emotion that seemed difficult to penetrate. The more intense the emotions, the more intense the thoughts, and so on. The way through it was to distance myself from the thoughts and emotions by recognizing that they were not me. While I was in the zone of meditation and daily readings, I would have recognized that this was happening to me as it was happening. I would have focused on my breath, visualized the emotion as a passing wave that needed to come and go. I would have watched the feelings of hurt and confusion pass through me like a train in the night. I would have given them the time to truly be felt and picked myself up to continue my day.

But I was not in the place of a well-practiced balanced person. I had let myself slip out of the state of being that had kept me so at peace during this entire trying year. It was because of this that I didn't even recognize how heavily I dropped myself right in the middle of this pain. At the very least I would have known not to act in this state. I would have known to take a walk, call a friend, watch a show, do anything other than act on the emotions that were taking hold of an otherwise calm and confident personality. But then again, where would the story be if I had?

No, instead I called the one person who could not help at all, and actually only get hurt by my hurt; only get triggered by my trigger. He could only call to question who this person was before him who was acting in a way that had never shown itself before. Maybe I thought that he would ease my mind. Maybe I thought that calling a friend who was in a much more rational state would be 'beating around the bush.' I am not exactly sure why, after a lifetime of not being impulsive, I chose that moment to impulsively call him. Why the impulsivity? The pain, and the accompanied rush to make it go away.

The rest of the story is rather predictable. I called. I accused. I made it worse by claiming to have found proof in the details of a photo, that now looking back, I seriously question my perception and my intense desire to make my fearful thoughts right. Again, why the need to be right about something I so desperately didn't want to be right about? The pain, fear, triggers, and more pain. To make matters embarrassingly worse, I insisted that this call be done through facetime. The reason here was a meager attempt at being a detective. I thought if he were lying, I could spot the lie on his face and know how to proceed based on that information. My focus was on the narrative I had made up in my head, instead of on him or even myself.

By this point, the thoughts that were floating in my head turned to "maybe he has been projecting a lie this entire time." "Maybe his name is not even Jesse," and so on. My thoughts were not grounded in reality because the fear had taken over. *If I see his facial expressions through this lens*, I thought, *then maybe I can ascertain whether or not to believe him. Maybe after this I will get hired by the CIA as an international human lie detector. But first things first.*

What I didn't think through was how I would come across through Facetime. Accusatory jealousy mixed with ugly cry is apparently not my best look. Every word that he uttered I had a retort steeped in even more confusion. "Bern, please think about the kind of guy I am and if this matches up at all to the person you have been with for the past seven months." To which I replied something along the lines of "you never really know anyone." This statement made it very clear that there was absolutely nothing he could say that would ease my mind. I called him so that he could ease the pain, and then shunned him every time he tried. I momentarily forgot all the teachings from all of my gurus and years of mindfulness practices. Staying connected to those teachings helped me to stay grounded to the idea that this type of healing can only come from within. When you are blind to logic and stewing in emotion, the best way out is non-judgmental awareness of your state. Had I had just a bit more internal awareness at the time, my thoughts may have looked something like…

"Wow my heart is racing quite fast. My palms are sweaty and my muscles feel jumpy (that feeling when you just need to pace around the room). My inner thoughts are getting darker by the minute and they are beginning to scare me."

Next step could have been to address the above phenomena. "I will take a few deep breaths to help slow down my heart, but it's ok that my heart is fast right now."

"Instead of pacing back and forth, I will pace to the kitchen and make myself a cup of tea. That has been known to soothe me and will give me something to do with my hands."

"I will address the sweaty palms by stretching a bit. That will help me focus on my body instead of my thoughts. I will continue in this process until I feel a few steps past shock and able to think through things a bit more slowly."

When I hypothetically started to feel a bit more physically relaxed, I could have used the quietude to challenge my own thoughts with awareness of how my past was influencing the present. My reframed thoughts could have been challenged in this way.

"I feel petrified that I have been mistaken in assuming another person's state of being. I have been through a year wherein this type of questioning is to be expected. I came up with some very far reaching conclusions based on little evidence, highlighting this as a triggering event. I will bring awareness to the trigger and how I am feeling as a result. I will have compassion for myself at all times, but especially when I am coming from a place of fear. I will give myself as much time as I need to feel calm."

After this thought redirection, I could have taken the time that I just so compassionately gave myself and used it dial in on the moment. I could have focused on the here and now rather than past trauma and future fears, let myself not think, and instead focus my attention on my five senses. Essentially, I could have meditated in the way I was most versed. With that space, I even could have checked my own name to see if I also had a lingering outdated online profile. Which, to my chagrin, I did. Turns out, when you delete the app from your phone, it does not delete from the ethos. I could have come up with the exonerating proof on my own with just a little help from my prefrontal cortex.

I did not do any of the above and it gave me a fantastic wake up call. It woke me up to just how deeply triggers can run, and can sneak in without warning and slither into your psyche ever so quietly. I began thinking of The Intervention Fallacy (before I actually named it), and how it played a part in my seemingly automatic trigger to response speed.

Having a retrospective awareness of just how fast I went from trigger to reaction helped me to identify exactly where my work in personal growth needed to be. Even if all I did was delay the reaction following a trigger from a few seconds to a few minutes, then that would have been amazing growth. Victor Frankl said, "Between stimulus and response there is a space. In that space is our power to choose a response. In our response lies our growth and our freedom." Yes, Victor!! Thank you for putting it so succinctly. Maybe one day we will all get to a place where triggers no longer, well, trigger us. Until then, our freedom lies in creating space between trigger and response.

I like to practice what I preach in my therapy office. When I advise meditation, I like to make sure that I have an ongoing meditation practice myself. When I discover a new mindfulness technique, I make sure that I give that technique a personal whirl before telling a patient about it. And when possible, I will begin the mindfulness technique with a patient right there in the office, so that when they go home, they are more inclined to imbibe the practice into their daily lives because it feels less foreign. Depending on where the patient is in his or her meditational journey, I tend to start with the breath. Every breath is an opportunity to reconnect with yourself and your state of being. Once a practice of deep "belly" breathing is established, we can begin to utilize the breath for self regulation and especially for creating space.

It is amazing to me how many instances can be mitigated by using your breath. Can you hear me deep breathing through these lines of text? I am doing it right now. Every thought as I type is accompanied by a slow rhythmic breath that helps me to find clarity in the words and profundity in the content. When someone comes into my office asking for help with anger management, we start with the breath. Anxiety management, we start with the breath. Stress management, definitely the breath. And on and on. I have met with people experiencing severely debilitating panic attacks, and after a few sessions of primarily breath work, they experience a significant improvement. Your breath is always there for you one hundred percent of the time.

Breath work is the start to spiritual practices, as well as self regulation. If you have not yet tried it, the tenants are simple. Put your hands on your belly. Go ahead, do it right now. Draw your breath into your hand, thereby bringing your breath to your belly instead of your chest. Feel your hand slowly rise and fall with your belly. As your lung capacity increases, you will feel the need to take less breaths because there is more oxygen readily available. Slowly and softly in and out, preferably through your nose. Take note of that quiet moment between the in and out breaths. There is a very subtle moment in time, after every exhale, that the body pauses before inhaling again. That is a place of such beautiful stillness. Anyone who has been trained to fire a gun or shoot an arrow knows that moment as the most opportune time to fire. Breath equals stillness.

In this situation with Jesse, I did eventually find my stillness. It took a full day of processing and a phone call to Rachel who said, "Oh, you are so triggered. Remember this is Jesse! The guy who drove all the way out to Pennsylvania and then to Long Island to meet your friends. This sounds nothing like him and you need to connect to the part of yourself that knows that through and through."

"Then why does my heart hurt so bad right now?" I said.

"Because you have had a lifetime of ups and downs. Because the downs have a way of lingering and piercing when you least expect it. Because you fell very much in love with a person who deserves your love, and you trust a person who deserves your trust, and you feel vulnerable and exposed as a result. But that vulnerability is why you are able to love in the first place. Trust in your ability to work through those hard feelings. They will go away, but the joyful intrinsic you will remain."

"But how can I trust in my ability to work through hard feelings if my ability just failed me miserably?"

"Are you still doing your morning meditations and guru readings?"

Rachel nailed it. I hadn't been and I appreciated the very actionable advice that I could begin immediately. I centered myself and got a good night's sleep. Jesse and I were able to work through it all the next day when I graciously brought up the subject by saying, "Remember that time when I was all accusatory based on essentially nothing? So glad *that's* in the past."

"You rehearsed that line didn't you?"

"Yes, yes I did."

My apology was clumsy at the start, but bled into a meaningful conversation. I took into account how he must have been feeling. One minute he was enjoying his Sunday with friends and family, and the next he was watching his girl-friend unravel in an accusatory manner for something that was no fault of his own.

"It was confusing because that is just so not like you." he said.

I explained the intervention fallacy and specifically how I planned to keep it in check. Overall, there are certain emotions that are meant to be kept raw. We can't really work through them until we rub up against them. I couldn't work through loving a person and then questioning my resulting fragility until I loved someone and questioned my resulting fragility. Luckily, I was in love with a person who could be strong enough to hear me out, compassionate enough to understand where it came from, and loving enough to see through it all.

POST-DIVORCE
INTERNAL LOVE CONFLICT

People talk about the battle between the head and the heart frequently, but with post-divorce it is like that issue has been put on steroids.

I felt in my insides, whatever my insides were, that I found a person who made my heart sing. I never knew that someone so different from me could be so much like me. Jesse was so rugged, and masculine, and sporty, and his approach to things was just so male. He saw a rope swing and saw hours of fun, I saw a rope swing and saw what ifs. He found a broken part and saw a fun puzzle, I saw a headache and an ever growing list of things to do. And still there was the shock that a person could approach life as similarly as I did. The polarity that exists between his approach and mine gave a feeling of completeness. It was a tackle-the-world with interdependence type practicality, mixed with passion and tenderness. What was even better was that this feeling came with the experience of a spiritually lifted 40-year-old. I had never been more in touch with myself and what I needed. I had never been able to read a person and his needs so well, and those needs felt like a pleasure to fill.

But then there was the head. The one that wants to argue and wait for the other shoe to drop. The one that says "forever" didn't work the first time so why give my heart to a person again? It could be possible that we were meant to spend a given amount of time with a person while it made sense, but certainly not forever.

The scariest look for any divorced person is the one from a person still living in a marriage that keeps going beyond the expiration date "for the kids." It's like an ex-smoker who smells smoke and is more offended than anyone else in the room. It's a place of stagnation that we never want to find ourselves in again. But, there is a way to put a positive spin on this one, too. The romance of non-commitment. No marriage, no wedding bands, no promissory note, means that every day you are with someone is by choice. You are not staying with him because of the overly optimistic promise that you made years ago to stay connected to a person forever. The head can romance the fuck out of this situation to prove its point. Long term commitment doesn't make sense for two people who are constantly growing and evolving and changing. How do we know we will grow in the same direction?

In the beginning (that term is relative but just go with it), Jesse would put my face in his hands and say "Please don't change." On his couch, with the soulful voice of Amy Winehouse coming from his old-fashioned record player, the two of us lay so close and so still. The crackle of the vinyl brought a realness to the music that cannot be achieved through any other means. He caught the moment in his gesture as he conveyed the sense that we both had. It was the sense that says "this person is too good. Please don't let this be a mirage, a person on his/her best behavior who couldn't possibly be kept up for a significant length of time. Please actually be the person that I'm seeing. It would break my heart to be this in love with a version of you that isn't real."

I knew where he was coming from, but I just couldn't agree to it. As softly and with as much compassion as I could muster, I simply said no can do. I evolved way too much to make a promise like that. I could feel myself growing at that time with such intensity and ferocity that I could not predict what would come out the other side.

"Just see me," I said in my most primal attempt at direct-ness. "If you see me, the part of me that is at my core, you will see the part that doesn't change. My situation changes daily, my home will change, as will the car that I drive. The thoughts, actions, and even hobbies that consume my time are ephemeral and will evolve without warning. That is the part of me that I place no guarantee. Actually, if I were to guarantee anything, it is that all of us are more prone to change than we are to stay the same. To see the part that doesn't change you will need to dig deep."

He heard that and breathed it in. He then gave me one of those kisses that are epic and electrifying. The kind that romance novels are based upon. He held on to that kiss with strength and passion and only responded with, "I love you, Bern."

What else could he say or do? He laid his fears out on the table in the simplest terms. "Please be who you appear to be." I could have just given him the easy answer that I knew he wanted to hear. But instead I took him on the more com-plicated path filled with depth and curve balls. The truth was harder to explain but brought with it more rewards. It was a way to say that my hobbies may change, but if you love the insides of me, you will also love how the outsides present themselves in ever changing ways. Today's foosball obsession will be tomorrow's emerging knack for knitting. But to really know me meant seeing that underneath those hobbies was an insatiable curiosity. That was the part that will last, even if the foosball table collects dust. Know the hobbies, but truly love the values that brought the hobbies to fruition.

In relationships, we might be impressed with a person's ability to sail a boat, but if that is the reason we love him, what are we left with if he breaks an arm and can no longer sail? We can be impressed by hobbies, but not in love be-cause of them. If we cling on to the ephemeral parts of a person, that love will be fleeting at best. Plus, we would miss out on the best and juiciest parts of a person. We would miss out on the lovely underbelly that takes inquisitive eyes to see. Jesse would have missed out on my curiosity and I would have missed out on his thoughtfulness. It is such a comfort for me to know that he might not always continue his love for mountain biking, but his thoughtful nature will be everlasting. We both dug deep. We saw the parts of the other that truly don't change. Those parts were truly a joy to find, know, and love.

So in answering his question, I took him on a more winding road. I challenged him to suck at the marrow of human existence and his response was to hold me tighter. In many ways, we spoke very different languages. He was direct and succinct while I was verbose and colorful. His spiritual path has been subtle and undefined. He hasn't studied under the same gurus, read the same books, or sat in the same silence. But he was able to bridge that gap by listening to the only truth I knew how to give.

I am me. That's all I have ever been. The head and the heart will continue to battle it out, but in the end, none of it matters. I will be there to see certain parts change, and others remain the same. He will continue to be baffled by my circuitous manner of answering questions, but will stick with me until my heart brings it home. We will both be there through the thick of it, leaning closer as the record plays on.

Drop Your Ego In Summation

- Take that stronger you and see what develops because of it.

- Understand that the practices you have put in place to help you feel better need to stay in place. You are not better than your practices.

- You are not your thoughts.

- What is the part of you that doesn't change? Breath into that place and stay connected to it. Indulge in the core of who you are.

CHAPTER SEVEN

FORGIVENESS

Sand the Floor

"Bless the energy you leave behind. Anything you blame you are stuck with." Area Shanti

Forgiveness is not your seventh and final spiritual step. It is actually an amalgam of each step. This behemoth of a concept is one that takes practice, awareness, and understanding; and calls upon all the other work you have been doing to truly come to the surface in a meaningful way.

It is very similar to the scene in Karate Kid when Mr. Miyagi says, "Show me sand the floor," and Danielson is able to utilize all the work he had been doing up to that point. He didn't realize it but he was building muscle memory in order to swiftly perform the karate chopping actions demanded of him by Mr. Miyagi. That is what you have been doing thus far in increasing your awareness of the spiritual steps. Forgiveness is like a muscle that needs to be trained and strengthened while simultaneously in use.

To review what you have been doing thus far in terms of forgiveness, we will walk through each of the six steps you have traveled. You began your journey with the first step which was to gather your resources. Forgiveness takes strength of character, and the first way to find that strength is to gather your resources to remind you where your strength lies, both outside of you and within you. Especially when there is a heaping pile of dogshit being thrown at your door each day. Your team, your emotional tools, and your inner compass will help you to build that forcefield that will keep the negativity at a distance so that you can heal and rebuild.

Next, you needed to learn how to handle those waves of emotions, because no part of this works in a straight line. You have honed your skill of managing waves of emotion because there will be days when forgiveness will come more naturally, and others will be more of a struggle. Your understanding and awareness of these waves of emotion will help you to harness the right energy at the right time. Like a windmill harnesses energy differently on the windy versus calm days, you will do the same by harnessing your emotions to work for you.

Your relationship autopsy will help you to see that there are so many things you are forgiving here. It's not just him or her, it's also yourself, circumstances, life, and even the construct of marriage. Each will have its turn.

Next, you learned acceptance, which is the cornerstone of forgiveness. It helps us to not only see the reality of the situation, but also that people and constructs have limitations. As you enter into situations, you do so knowing that no person is perfect, and no commitment is perfect. Accepting these limitations will help you to see the fallible nature therein, thereby paving the way toward empathic understanding of various indiscretions. Upon accepting your suffering, you will be able to find meaning in it, thereby nurturing your higher vibration and emanating it onto others.

How does moving on help with forgiveness? I am a firm believer in old, often told advice. The saying, "The best way to get over someone is to get under someone else," is, well, more about forgiveness than it is about sex. Certain hard feelings are pacified as you watch that water go right under that bridge. And of course, it doesn't have to be about a relationship at all, but about getting absorbed in something, anything, that takes your breath away. This will help you to prioritize where you want your flow of energy.

Next came step number six. You have been challenged to drop that ego. Get out of your damn head. It can get messy in there. Shed those attachments and create space for the inner you to emerge. If you are going to run the marathon of forgiveness, you will need to drop that added weight. Run, Forest, run.

Just as Danielson had more to do after fixing Mr. Miyage's house and defying child labor laws, there are a few more exercises that will maximize your process of forgiveness.

First, understand that forgiveness has nothing to do with the offender, nor does there need to be an offender present. Sometimes people need to forgive someone for dying, or getting sick, or other actions that are no fault in nature. Other times, forgiveness is needed for repeat offenses which would be counterintuitive if the forgiveness had anything to do with the offender. Instead, it is about reaping the therapeutic benefits for you and those around you.

Can I get a shout out to Jesus? He was the ultimate iconoclast and the reigning champion on forgiveness. He brought forgiveness into the world like an elephant on main street. Gentle and kind, but huge and unmistakable. His message was earth-shatteringly clear. Forgiveness breeds lightness and paves the way to living according to your intentions. Thanks JC! Couldn't have done it without you.

Pace yourself on your forgiveness journey. It is a process that can take any amount of time to complete. The idea is not to race to complete it, but to just be somewhere along its winding road. You will know that you are coming to the road's completion when you are able to think about the person or event and it conjures up little to no emotion. When it truly feels like something that is in your past and remembered, but not continuing to hold weight. The examples that follow will help you to drop the weight and, in turn, feel the lightness.

GRATITUDE

The first actionable part of forgiveness is gratitude. I know, the last thing recently-divorced people want is someone telling them to be thankful for what they have. It sounds like a forced version of a Hallmark card that no one wanted to buy. One with a picture of a lost puppy on the front, and the inside jacket that reads "Congratulations on your divorce, now you can be thankful for the shrapnel left behind in its wake." The platitudes and advice are well intended but often hollow and misdirected. It's ok to shun them out. You need for the thoughts circling in your brain to be purposeful. Therefore it is perfectly ok, in fact beneficial, to be selective about the thoughts that get to rent space in your mind. The people who want to sugar coat the situation mean well, but have no idea what you are going through, and are the least of your problems. Treat them, and all well-intended nosy bodies, with compassion and move on.

Once you have transgressed from the surface level minutia, it will be time to find your deeper place. It is there that you will encounter incredibly effective gratitude. Be still. Breath. And go deep.

Gratitude begins with questions. What do you have? Truly and honestly what are the important things in your life and do you have them? I am going to bet that you do. I am going to bet that at this moment you can call a person who is always willing to hear you out. If there are kids involved, that is a no brainer. They might make life extremely difficult, especially in a divorce situation, but you have them. They are an endless source of love on both the giving and receiving end, and are a continual source of gratitude overflow. How is that breath? Is it softly, gently, and quietly bringing oxygen and life energy to every cell in your body? Can you feel its rhythm course through you like a trusted metronome intent on keeping you in a forward motion? There is always something to be thankful for. I would be saying this to a person in solitary confinement at a state penitentiary, so I will certainly say it to you.

There are always aspects of your current surroundings that you can be thankful for. Are you holding on to a cozy blanket? Are you thankful for the cup of tea in your hand? When you think about your day, what were the moments that stood out for you? Did the sun touch your skin? Did you appreciate the laughter in the breakroom? As you make a practice of this, you will begin to note the times that you are especially grateful. With practice comes mastery. Some find it helpful to keep a gratitude journal, others find it more helpful to place gratefulness reminders throughout their day. Do what works for you, but know that this step cannot be skipped. It is an integral part of forgiveness.

Gratitude works on many levels. Not only does it set your mind in a state of fullness, but it also changes your mood in a way that can be both uplifting and freeing. There is a reason gratitude is a part of almost every religion and spiritual philosophy ever recorded. So much of our lives are spent pursuing one goal or another; or in some cases, it's a person, object, or title. Gratitude reverses that process. It teaches us to be thankful for the things we already have. It reminds us that we are enough. You, unmarried, starting over, beautiful you, are enough!

CRANE KICK

Let's move on to the Miyagi crane kick of forgiveness. Thank goodness I am not going to ask you to leap off one load-bearing foot, and deliver an effective strike with that same foot. But therapeutically speaking, it is proportionate. As your self-nominated therapist en-text, I strongly urge you to write a letter to your ex if it is a situation wherein you will need to continue a relationship with said person. If there are kids involved, you will need to continue your relationship with this person forever. If there were miscommunications during the marriage, there will certainly be more post-marriage, plus the never-ending milieu of confusion, anger, resentment, etc. These are difficult emotions to wade through on a good day, but given the stressors of life and the amount of effort we as a collective whole put into child rearing, we owe it to ourselves to bring the best energy we can into the situation. Hence, bring those arms up in a "V" and position yourself for the crane kick.

If, when you look at your ex, you see the reason for the break, it will feel like a dagger through your heart every time. Make no mistake, this is the energy you will feel, and therefore bring into the room. Your body will internalize it, your heart will feel it, and your words will reflect it. Looking at a person with scorn has the potential to eat through your insides like a cancer and leave nothing but stench in its wake. Any interaction you have with this person will come as a result of this resentment-filled foundation, and your children will pick up on it.

So now, it's time to take that spirituality you've been working on and use it to write a letter.

Writing this letter will not help you to wake up one day in a state of complete forgiveness, but it is a step in that direction. A commitment to take a step toward something does not guarantee the end result, but it sets a stage of forward motion which is generally what every divorced person wants. How do I move from the wreckage of divorce to a place where I feel like I have moved on? This is the question that resonates deeply and can be applied to any part of the divorce process. Whether you are in the pre-separation stages and contemplating what divorce might look like, are years past having papers signed, or somewhere in the middle, you can always take a step closer to reconciling with what it all meant to you.

Since forgiveness is a process that never really ends, doesn't work in a straight line, and can circle back at any time, let's just proceed. You can come back to this step as many times as you would like because it will be your new foundation. Here is the formula:

1. Write a letter to your ex.
2. Include two examples, one of a memory of you, ex and your kids, family, or community. Make it a good one that makes you smile (even if the happy memories make you cry even more than the sad ones... I know... I get it). The second memory is of just the two of you.
3. Seal the letter and choose whether or not to send it. Sending it is just a by-product of the exercise and is not needed, but may help your ex see what you are doing and inspire him or her to do the same. But as you know, I don't give a shit about your ex, this letter is for you.
4. Picture one of these two memories every time you see your ex. Choose the memory that best fits the context and your state of being.

This letter can be written using your own template; but if it is difficult to start, you can read mine and use it as a jumping point. This exercise is so important, so cathartic, and so integral to the tone you set for yourself as you move forward that I really don't care how you do it, just as long as you get it done.

Example #1.

Dear Ex,

When I see you and when I talk to you, I will have the following memories in my mind as a reminder that we were not always what we are now. We were once a connected, unified team doing our best to take on the world. As the memories fade, and the stories get rewritten, and hindsight gets jaded, I will not let either of these memories become tampered or mistaken. I will keep them crystal clear to be called upon frequently as an accurate account of what happened on one day, from one perspective, during the course of our marriage.

The first was on a random Sunday night. We were in a dark closet at the end of the hallway hiding from our children in an oddly competitive game of hide and seek. You said something funny and I couldn't help but belly laugh. I have no idea what you said, for the life of me I would love to know that detail, but I don't. It must not matter. You cupped your hand around my mouth to keep me from laughing so hard that I would blow up our spot. I could feel your hands on my mouth as your body shook from trying to contain your own laughter. In the darkness and surrounded by suitcases and bed linens, I leaned on you, you leaned on me, we laughed so hard we almost fell over, and we still won that fucking game.

The second memory is of you and me, a rented sailboat, and a bottle of champagne.

This is how I want to remember us, so this is how I choose to in this moment. These memories do not deny all the other stuff. All of that is real and has its place. But in going forward, and in trying to bring the best energy that I can to our current situation, this will be where my head is at. These two memories will remain untouched and untainted. They embody why I loved you, and they will remain a piece of me forever.

And that is all. No signature necessary. Sending optional.

A colleague of mine told one of her patients to just pretend to be highly medicated every time she interacted with the difficult people in her life. She told her to basically periodically take a trip to happy town to help her become less aggravated by things she could not control. As simple and easy as this may sound, it is actually an advanced method of compartmentalization and is highly effective. So, if the above exercise falls short for you in handling your ex, I advise you to pretend to be as high as possible for each and every one of your interactions. You may not get anything done, but at the very least your stress levels will remain pacified, and since you are only pretending to be high, it won't leave you with a hangover.

THE SHOUT

I have mentioned that sometimes knowing something comes at first like a tickle. It seems like a nudge in the night that tells you to pay attention to the warning signs. When those signs are ignored, it comes on stronger as the nudge turns to a headache. And when the headache is ignored, it hits you like a panic attack in the middle of Times Square. I had the presence of mind to pay attention at this stage. This nudge, that turned into a shout, helped me to put into motion the changes needed to set my soul back on its course. My body knew before I did that the particular course was just not right for me.

This happened countless times throughout my marriage and throughout my life—these bodily and cosmic interruptions that threw me off course only to set it right again. It was only in recent years that I have been becoming more and more aware of them and ready to make changes at their arrival. However, there were times when messages were there and I didn't pay attention. Those times when my body failed me, were they just coincidence? Those times when things seemed off, was that a nudge? Was that a reason to begin making marital changes? I don't think so, but interpretations are quite subjective. Could someone else have interpreted them as the beginning stages of putting the fork in the road? Who am I to judge?

The added layer to my forgiveness was in the awareness of *his* nudges. What were his times that his soul sent messages to him urging him to reconsider his course? Did he receive it as a whisper? How long did he ignore those whispers only to come home to a place in his life that felt foreign?

What did those whispers turn into as they breathed out the fire that refused to be ignored? How many times did he try to convince himself that the nagging voice in his head was only a fleeting distraction? I can only imagine how much pain this must have caused him. The pain of ignoring the nudge for an undetermined amount of time must have paled in comparison to the shout that got him to pay attention. Divorce causes pain for the people involved. He did not escape the pain of divorce and would have avoided it if it were at all possible for him. But because of the nudge and then the shout, the whisper, and then the panic attack, the seeing and the undoing, avoiding divorce was no longer possible for him.

It was Maya Angelu who said, "When you know better, you do better." There are times when we know better and times when we don't. There are times when we know how to read the signs and times when we feel lost and misguided. The most confusing part is that it is very difficult to differentiate the two. Which was that point that he didn't know better, and which was the point that he knew better so well that it just couldn't be ignored?

I may not have the amount of compassion that it takes to fully walk in his shoes. I vehemently disagreed with his decision for us to separate at the time that he made it. I believed that there was another way through to making us strong. But in the end, that is really just a difference of opinion. The areas that made us click (strongly opinionated) were also the areas that created the great divide. A long time ago I prayed to God to give me a sign and she did. She told me that he was doing me a favor, and I do have enough compassion to see the wisdom in that. Maybe that was the last time I would have to vehemently disagree with a person about a decision so huge. It could be that the favor he did for me was to unleash the emotions that led to personal transformation. He stepped back and I emerged happier, stronger, and burning brighter than I ever thought possible. That certainly was not because of him, but I will never deny that I am grateful for the many twists of fate that got me to that place.

Understanding your ex's side of the story will help you to gain compassion because it involves evoking empathy. This will help you to understand the differences between you and your ex, and to see them from a different viewpoint. When you can truly see your relationship from your ex's lens and then actively choose to forgive based on that view, you are choosing to put empathy into motion. You are choosing compassion. This loop needs to take place for all the players in your marriage, including yourself, your preconceived notions, and the marriage itself. Forgiveness does not have a myopic lens. The more components that you can break apart, bring out into the sun, and turn around in the light to look at from all different angles, the more steps you will take on your road to forgiveness.

Do you see how this is a choice? It takes work, practice, and may feel uncomfortable at first. But the product of forgiveness is lightness, and you owe it to yourself to walk into your next chapter unburdened by the weight of the last one. For this, I turn to The Buddha "Our sorrows and wounds are healed only when we touch them with compassion." Let's heal some wounds, and see the sorrows, and be touched by the soft glow left behind by compassion. It will do us all some good.

The Lightness

Now that you are on the road to forgiveness it is time to truly feel the lightness. The sun will feel just a little bit warmer and the leaves will look just a little bit brighter. Those close to you will be appreciated in a deeper way because they helped you, in some way, along your journey.

On a beautiful summer day, over a year past marital separation, I was making my famous rainbow vegetable plate as a large group of kids were playing outside. I was chopping my vegetables while surrounded by friends, both old and new, doing their portion of busy work. The most wonderful part about a kitchen island is the number of sous chefs that can fit around it. The breeze blew in from the open windows as the sound of many knives on cutting boards sliced through the air. Jesse was hard at work making a chimichurri sauce, Ellie was taking yet another lesson on how to open a bottle of wine, while others prepared the kabobs. No one seemed rushed at all because the preparations were the party. There was no other moment to get to because we were already in the one unfolding.

A song about watermelon sugar came on the speaker system. The catchy-ness of the song had a contagious nature as everyone started unconsciously bopping to it. It was more of a head dance as the other extremities were still used for chopping. When the chorus came on everyone started singing using an array of celery stalks and wooden spoons for microphones.

This moment was quite similar to many other moments that transpired that summer. It could have gone unnoticed. It could have slipped from my long term memory along with the cascade of so many others before it. But it didn't. Kai didn't let that happen. She leaned into my chopping space and said, "This is it, Bernie. This is the reward."

She told me so many times that things would get better. She told me that divorce was murky and scary at first. She identified with the fright like a soldier who had seen that battleground before. She assured me that not only would I feel ok, but that things would actually get better than they were pre-divorce. I didn't necessarily believe her at the time, but I kept the faith. She then pointed out, with arrows and underlined moments, exactly when the rewards were coming in. "Right now, Bernie, feel this right now, this moment was brought to you by your next chapter."

She was right. The lightness appears from all angles. It comes from within and shines its brightest when it is free from the clouds that can block its journey. Be it time, effort, awareness, or spiritual enlightenment, I saw my way through the clouds and into a freer headspace.

I once heard that divorce is like getting into a car accident every single day. There is something true about this analogy. Every morning you wake up and position yourself for the car wreck. You remind yourself that you can handle the details and the smoking engine. You give a sigh of relief that your loved ones are ok as well as your physical being. As you handle the police report, and the other driver, and assess the no fault nature of the wreck, you look around at the traffic that is angling to get by you. The police officer asks questions about the moments leading up to the wreck to assess if it could have been prevented. Your answers don't change anything about the reality. You spend your day on the side of the road as you are visited by those that love you and give you support and encouragement. Then you wake up the next morning and do it all over again.

The lightness comes when you are able to walk away from the crash. At some point, that day will become yesterday. As you continue to walk, it dissolves further and further into your growing collection of yesterdays. It doesn't come when the journey is complete. It comes during the times that you choose to feel it. The reminders will help, but the only one who can truly feel it is you. The only one that can join in the chorus holding a vegetable microphone, is you.

I didn't always have Kai around, so I needed to become aware of the lightness myself. I needed to catch those moments, hold them up to the light, and appreciate them from all angles. I needed to bop my head in unison with those around me just because it felt right. I needed to take my vegetable plate out to the kids because that was my next right step. And on and on through the turbulence, stress, struggle, and reward. It was all happening anyway, but the lightness shone through each step with a glow seen by anyone watching.

Forgiveness In Summation

- Review your progress thus far. You will need all the strength you have mustered.

- Be grateful every day.

- Put gratefulness into action by articulating your appreciation.

- Walk in his or her shoes. Compassion is the key to letting go.

- When the light shines in, let it.

CONCLUSION

In Japanese folklore, there is a legend of a renowned shogun warrior who broke his favorite tea bowl. He sent it away for repairs, and when he received it back, he was disappointed with the metal staples used to hold it together. He was determined to fix his tea bowl in a more useful and elegant way.

He asked a craftsman to try a new technique. One that would highlight the cracks instead of hide them. So, the craftsman mixed the glue with a resin made of gold. When he returned the bowl it was back to its functioning form but this time with streaks of gold, which added beauty to the overall aesthetic.

From this story came the art of Kintsugi, or the philosophy of embracing the flawed or imperfect. It celebrates the beauty in broken things and changing conditions. The knocks, the breaks, and the shattered pieces are part of the culmination of human existence that can be seen as the added value to a functioning form.

All of us have always been a functioning form, but now we have added value. We have felt these breaks and have picked the pieces up off the floor. We have found the golden resin to add to our glue by reaching for the lesson in all of it. Now our breaks and tears have become the beautiful binding glue that holds our pieces together, stronger than before.

The fusion of my parts, the pieces of my bowl, were just about finished and looking almost back to their functioning form. I held the last two pieces in my hand and looked for one more drop of golden resin. I brought myself back to the room I was in, and saw that the pieces were that which stood before me, and the golden glue was the bond that we shared.

"Mama, look at this dance I just made up," Mavis said with a piece of pizza still in her mouth. She got up from the table to show Avery and me her new favorite groove. The three of us were eating lunch at our favorite pizza place. It was a small local joint with refurbished church pews as seats and an old-fashioned Pacman game console in the corner. The old wood of the pews brought with them a certain sanctity and witness to a million prayers, while the smell of the pizza was a ubiquitous reminder that they sat in a new setting now. The combination of old meeting new had a synergy to it that was palpable. Children from all over town flocked to this pizza joint and its neighboring ice cream parlor for more than just food. It was for the feeling of simple times and effortless pleasures. The kids knew it as their post-beach destination, and adults knew it as the place that reminded them of childhood.

We sat up on our pews poised to watch Mavis' dance show as we finished our napoleon slices. She began with a hula dance and then plunged into a sumo wrestler's stance. We tried to contain our laughter but a few giggles found their way through the corner of our mouths. We were uncertain if she was trying to make us laugh or seriously trying to dance. As soon as she saw one smile, unable to hide her mercurial nature, she delved deeper into sumo style, and began adding arm movements. Avery and I tend to fall off things when we laugh too hard, and this one had us falling off our pew in seconds. Like a master ringleader, Mavis read her crowd and added a shuffle to her dance, bringing her around the room in a Polynesian dance fusion. She rounded out her act with a leaping pirouette and fell jovially onto my lap, completing our circle of falling laughter.

For a moment the room disappeared. All I could see was the three of us, feeling like a family. After months of upturned moments that felt suddenly misplaced, this one was undoubtedly earned. It was the culmination of so much love and so much reshaping. I reshaped my idea of what family looks like, and feels like. I took them in my arms in celebration because the three of us were enough. In our own, girlie, made up, take charge way, we were us. My laughter turned to happy tears and grateful joy.

"Do it again," Avery said as Mavis jumped up in gleeful acquiescence.

Avery and I sat back to watch the show play out once more, and then once more after that. The scene of the three of us charging through the world as one family plays out over and over from the inside out. The three of us have always been enough. Our broken pieces along the way gave us the chance to bind our parts back together in a golden and beautiful way.

Once I could truly see our version of enough, I could never go back to thinking there needed to be more. Once you get to a place of knowing, you can never go back to not knowing. Every step along your spiritual path is a step toward knowing. With each step taken, the old steps fall away because you never want to go back. Your path goes up toward a destination unknown. Spirituality becomes your process by which you ascend in forward motion, one step at a time, continuously grounded while also moving forward. The steps fall away unnoticed behind you because they became a part of you as you consumed them.

The push that you needed to jumpstart your spiritual ascension was so much less important than the ascension itself. That which transforms us was never as important as the transformation itself. It could have been a divorce or a tsunami. The details were less important than the fortitude that you used to turn the tsunami into your personal metamorphosis.

It is time now to come bursting through those flames. When you do the work, truly and honestly take on the challenges that your particular human existence has provided, you will break through the wall that kept the best parts of you contained. With those parts untethered, you become free to relearn your new, magnificent self.

In the most practical sense, I am the one who gets it all done. I am the man of the house and woman of the house now. I am the one who fixes the sink. I am the one who fires up the grill and kills the spider. I am the one who throws my jean shorts on so that I can check the strange noise coming from the first floor in the middle of the night. When I find it to be a shutter that's come loose, I am the one who strings it up, barefoot and strong. I do this with confidence and bravery like I've never had before. I have learned to stand tall when I used to cower. I have learned to grow bigger when I used to rely on someone else to be the brave one. I don't pretend that I could defend the home against an invader, but I do wield a very powerful cell phone and I'm not afraid to use it. I've had to take on both roles. The feminine came to me so freely and easily, and the masculine has taken some growing. But in the end that's the point. Growth and balance and coming out the other side a stronger, more assured and confident person.

This is true for the impractical side too. The side that comes from high and influences all we touch, was also led by me. Because whichever part of the source speaks the loudest, I was receptive to hear it. That carries its own comfort because I am the one who will ultimately always be with me. I am the one whispering, "He's doing you a favor." I am the one knowing which direction to turn. I am the one confused and baffled and I am also the one holding the compass at due north, knowing exactly what my due north is. I am the one stroking my hair and telling myself it's ok if you sleep, it's also ok if you don't. I am the one falling apart and I am the one gathering the pieces together and formulating a new life in a new chapter. I am the one rising.

I am here to tell you that you can be both. Be the one who is breaking down and also the one who is repairing. Be the one smashing the plate and also the one making the mosaic from the pieces.

I have a quote hanging on the wall of my office. It says, "Your wounds will heal you," by Paulo Coelho. I believe that quote to be true for all who come to my office, because just by being there in a therapeutic setting, each person has signed up for a deeper look into what ails them and what cures them.

You have done this. You have gotten past some of the biggest flames already. You are still breathing the smokey air because new challenges always arise. But the point here is not to steer clear of those challenges, but to know that you can handle each one. You can handle the snow that hits you in the face, you can handle the newness of foreign situations, you can handle that question that comes from your child's sad eyes, and you can handle the next break that life throws you. These breaks add to your beauty and your overall value.

Along your journey remember the words from Faith. Happiness is a state of being. Moving on is a state of being. Starting over is a state of being. Living in the past will keep you feeling vengeful and unrequited. Thoughts of the future will bring on more stress than is necessary. When you bring to mind that your state of being is your choice, your actions will follow in alignment with that choice. Let your actions reflect your true intentions and you will be amazed at how the universe begins to work in your favor. You will see more coincidences, more serendipity, and more moments of peace. The energy you are cultivating now is of a higher vibration and it is where you will want to stay.

I have seen these changes in myself and I have told you my story. I have given you the honest naked truth of it all so that you can impart the wisdom that was handed to me from sources both living and gone. It is yours now. My journey is your journey because we are all connected now as we always have been. My support team is now yours as well. You can quote Faith, or Kai, or Bettie, Jesus, Buddha, Gandhi, Eckhart, and of course my mom. There has been a source using me as a conduit to bring their words to you. I found them comforting and I have a strong feeling you will too.

This source, the one that brings you to that higher place, is the part of you that is connected to your place of knowing. It is your 90-year-old self cheering you on, and your breath keeping you calm. It is your higher being, whichever one you subscribe to, sitting next to you and feeling it all with you. And sometimes it's just you. Your growing, healing, transforming self, making sure it will all be ok.

This part of you is going to get you through this. It is whispering to you, "I am here for you baby, every step of the way. I will cradle you and cry with you. Then I will dry those tears and help you take those steps forward. In fact, I already have."

It's your turn now.

Acknowledgements:

A long time ago I sat in disbelief at how supported I felt by those around me. These four women floored me with their support. It was their overflow of love that ran through my fingers and onto these pages. Barbara Purcell for giving me the best example of a mother that the world has ever known. Kristen Purcell for being my trailblazer, my touchstone, and my editor. Margot Raphael for lighting the path with kindness, faith, and strength. Carrie Herz for the Macbeth project, commute phone calls, and everything in between. Your support during my most difficult time will be forever in my heart.

Jill (Beaner) Ernst for being a constant source of friendship and inspiration, and yes even still, especially still. Jamie Intili for being so incredibly lovable, I could not have done it all without you. Robert (Pops) Purcell for telling me there's nothing I can't do. Mary Lougee, Kate Purcell, Justin Raphael, Bob Purcell, and Teresa Purcell, for a lifetime of encouragement, support, and love. Danielle Parmenter for being my plus one. Jaime Fernand for getting me in ways I don't get myself. Jodi Capman for showing me New Jersey. Barbara Coyle LCSW for being so darn good at your job. My engagement ring for sponsoring the production of this book (I do love me some irony).